Author's National Edition

THE WRITINGS OF
MARK TWAIN
VOLUME VII

This is the authorized Uniform Edition of all my books.

Mark Twain

RIDING A BUCKING BRONCHO

ROUGHING IT

BY MARK TWAIN
(Samuel L. Clemens)

IN TWO VOLUMES

VOL. I

HARPER & BROTHERS PUBLISHERS
NEW YORK AND LONDON

TO Calvin H. Higbie of California, an honest
man, a genial comrade, and a steadfast
friend, this book is inscribed by the author in
memory of the curious time when we two were
millionaires for ten days.

ILLUSTRATIONS

PREFATORY

THIS book is merely a personal narrative, and not a pretentious history or a philosophical dissertation. It is a record of several years of variegated vagabondizing, and its object is rather to help the resting reader while away an idle hour than afflict him with metaphysics, or goad him with science. Still, there is information in the volume; information concerning an interesting episode in the history of the Far West, about which no books have been written by persons who were on the ground in person, and saw the happenings of the time with their own eyes. I allude to the rise, growth, and culmination of the silver-mining fever in Nevada—a curious episode, in some respects; the only one, of its peculiar kind, that has occurred in the land; and the only one, indeed, that is likely to occur in it.

Yes, take it all around, there is quite a good deal of information in the book. I regret this very much, but really it could not be helped: information appears to stew out of me naturally, like the precious ottar of roses out of the otter. Sometimes it has seemed to me that I would give worlds if I could retain my facts; but it cannot be. The more I calk up the sources, and the tighter I get, the more I leak wisdom. Therefore, I can only claim indulgence at the hands of the reader, not justification.

THE AUTHOR.

CONTENTS

Contents

CHAPTER XIV.

CHAPTER XV.

CHAPTER XVI.

CHAPTER XVII.

CHAPTER XVIII.

CHAPTER XIX.

CHAPTER XX.

CHAPTER XXI.

Contents

CHAPTER XXX.

CHAPTER XXXI.

CHAPTER XXXII.

CHAPTER XXXIII.

CHAPTER XXXIV.

CHAPTER XXXV.

CHAPTER XXXVI.

CHAPTER XXXVII.

2

ROUGHING IT

CHAPTER I.

MY brother had just been appointed Secretary of Nevada Territory — an office of such majesty that it concentrated in itself the duties and dignities of Treasurer, Comptroller, Secretary of State, and Acting Governor in the Governor's absence. A salary of eighteen hundred dollars a year and the title of "Mr. Secretary," gave to the great position an air of wild and imposing grandeur. I was young and ignorant, and I envied my brother. I coveted his distinction and his financial splendor, but particularly and especially the long, strange journey he was going to make, and the curious new world he was going to explore. He was going to travel! I never had been away from home, and that word "travel" had a seductive charm for me. Pretty soon he would be hundreds and hundreds of miles away on the great plains and deserts, and among the mountains of the Far West, and would see buffaloes and Indians, and prairie dogs, and antelopes, and have all kinds of adventures, and maybe get hanged or scalped, and have ever such a fine time, and write home and tell us all about it, and be a hero. And he would see the gold mines and the silver mines, and maybe go about of an afternoon when his work was done, and pick up two or three pailfuls of shining slugs and nuggets of gold and silver on the hillside. And by and by he would become very rich, and return home by sea, and be able to talk as calmly about San Francisco and the ocean, and " the isthmus " as if it was nothing of any consequence to have seen those marvels face to face. What I suffered in contemplating his happiness, pen cannot describe. And so, when he offered me, in cold blood, the sublime position of private secretary under him, it appeared to me that the heavens and the earth passed away, and the firmament was rolled together as a scroll! I had nothing more to desire. My contentment was complete. At the end of an hour or two I was ready for the journey. Not much packing up was necessary, because we were going in the overland stage from the Missouri frontier to Nevada, and passengers were only allowed a small quantity of baggage apiece. There was no Pacific railroad in those fine times of ten or twelve years ago — not a single rail of it.

I only proposed to stay in Nevada three months — I had no thought of staying longer than that. I meant to see all I could that was new and strange, and then hurry home to business. I little thought that I would not see the end of that three-month pleasure excursion for six or seven uncommonly long years!

I dreamed all night about Indians, deserts, and silver bars, and in due time, next day, we took shipping at the St. Louis wharf on board a steamboat bound up the Missouri River.

We were six days going from St. Louis to " St. Joe" — a trip that was so dull, and sleepy, and eventless that it has left no more impression on my memory than if its duration had been six minutes instead of that many days. No record is left in my mind, now, concerning it, but a confused jumble of savage-looking snags, which we deliberately walked over with one wheel or the other; and of reefs which we butted and butted, and then retired from and climbed over in some softer place; and of sand-bars which we roosted on occasionally, and rested, and then got out our crutches and sparred over. In fact, the boat might almost as well have gone to St. Joe by land, for she was walking most of the time, anyhow — climbing over reefs and clambering over snags patiently and laboriously all day long. The captain said she was a " bully " boat, and all she wanted was more " shear " and a bigger wheel. I thought she wanted a pair of stilts, but I had the deep sagacity not to say so.

2*

CHAPTER II.

THE first thing we did on that glad evening that landed us at St. Joseph was to hunt up the stage-office, and pay a hundred and fifty dollars apiece for tickets per overland coach to Carson City, Nevada.

The next morning, bright and early, we took a hasty breakfast, and hurried to the starting-place. Then an inconvenience presented itself which we had not properly appreciated before, namely, that one cannot make a heavy traveling trunk stand for twenty-five pounds of baggage — because it weighs a good deal more. But that was all we could take — twenty-five pounds each. So we had to snatch our trunks open, and make a selection in a good deal of a hurry. We put our lawful twenty-five pounds apiece all in one valise, and shipped the trunks back to St. Louis again. It was a sad parting, for now we had no swallow-tail coats and white kid gloves to wear at Pawnee receptions in the Rocky Mountains, and no stove-pipe hats nor patent-leather boots, nor anything else necessary to make life calm and peaceful. We were reduced to a war-footing. Each of

us put on a rough, heavy suit of clothing, woolen
army shirt and " stogy " boots included; and into
the valise we crowded a few white shirts, some underclothing and such things. My brother, the Secretary, took along about four pounds of United States
statutes and six pounds of Unabridged Dictionary;
for we did not know—poor innocents—that such
things could be bought in San Francisco on one day
and received in Carson City the next. I was armed
to the teeth with a pitiful little Smith & Wesson's
seven-shooter, which carried a ball like a homœo-
pathic pill, and it took the whole seven to make a
dose for an adult. But I thought it was grand. It
appeared to me to be a dangerous weapon. It only
had one fault — you could not hit anything with it.
One of our " conductors " practiced awhile on a cow
with it, and as long as she stood still and behaved
herself she was safe; but as soon as she went to moving about, and he got to shooting at other things,
she came to grief. The Secretary had a small-sized
Colt's revolver strapped around him for protection
against the Indians, and to guard against accidents
he carried it uncapped. Mr. George Bemis was dismally formidable. George Bemis was our fellow-
traveler. We had never seen him before. He wore
in his belt an old original " Allen " revolver, such
as irreverent people called a " pepper-box." Simply drawing the trigger back, cocked and fired the
pistol. As the trigger came back, the hammer
would begin to rise and the barrel to turn over, and

B *

presently down would drop the hammer, and away would speed the ball.   To aim along the turning barrel and hit the thing aimed at was a feat which was probably never done with an "Allen" in the world.   But George's was a reliable weapon, nevertheless, because, as one of the stage-drivers afterwards said, " If she didn't get what she went after, she would fetch something else."   And so she did.   She went after a deuce of spades nailed against a tree, once, and fetched a mule standing about thirty yards to the left of it.   Bemis did not want the mule; but the owner came out with a double-barreled shot-gun and persuaded him to buy it, anyhow.   It was a cheerful weapon — the "Allen."   Sometimes all its six barrels would go off at once, and then there was no safe place in all the region round about, but behind it.

We took two or three blankets for protection against frosty weather in the mountains.   In the matter of luxuries we were modest — we took none along but some pipes and five pounds of smoking tobacco.   We had two large canteens to carry water in, between stations on the Plains, and we also took with us a little shot-bag of silver coin for daily expenses in the way of breakfast and dinners.

By eight o'clock everything was ready, and we were on the other side of the river.   We jumped into the stage, the driver cracked his whip, and we bowled away and left " the States " behind us.   It was a superb summer morning, and all the landscape was brilliant with sunshine.   There was a freshness

and breeziness, too, and an exhilarating sense of
emancipation from all sorts of cares and responsi-
bilities, that almost made us feel that the years we
had spent in the close, hot city, toiling and slaving,
had been wasted and thrown away. We were spinning along through Kansas, and in the course of an
hour and a half we were fairly abroad on the great
Plains. Just here the land was rolling — a grand
sweep of regular elevations and depressions as far as
the eye could reach — like the stately heave and
swell of the ocean's bosom after a storm. And
everywhere were cornfields, accenting with squares
of deeper green this limitless expanse of grassy
land. But presently this sea upon dry ground was
to lose its " rolling " character and stretch away for
seven hundred miles as level as a floor !

Our coach was a great swinging and swaying stage,
of the most sumptuous description — an imposing
cradle on wheels. It was drawn by six handsome
horses, and by the side of the driver sat the " conductor," the legitimate captain of the craft; for it
was his business to take charge and care of the
mails, baggage, express matter, and passengers.
We three were the only passengers, this trip. We
sat on the back seat, inside. About all the rest of
the coach was full of mail bags — for we had three
days' delayed mails with us. Almost touching our
knees, a perpendicular wall of mail matter rose up
to the roof. There was a great pile of it strapped
on top of the stage, and both the fore and hind

boots were full. We had twenty-seven hundred
pounds of it aboard, the driver said — "a little for
Brigham, and Carson, and 'Frisco, but the heft of it
for the Injuns, which is powerful troublesome 'thout
they get plenty of truck to read." But as he just then
got up a fearful convulsion of his countenance which
was suggestive of a wink being swallowed by an
earthquake, we guessed that his remark was intended
to be facetious, and to mean that we would unload
the most of our mail matter somewhere on the Plains
and leave it to the Indians, or whosoever wanted it.

We changed horses every ten miles, all day long,
and fairly flew over the hard, level road. We
jumped out and stretched our legs every time the
coach stopped, and so the night found us still viva-
cious and unfatigued.

After supper a woman got in, who lived about
fifty miles further on, and we three had to take turns
at sitting outside with the driver and conductor.
Apparently she was not a talkative woman. She
would sit there in the gathering twilight and fasten
her steadfast eyes on a mosquito rooting into her
arm, and slowly she would raise her other hand till
she had got his range, and then she would launch a
slap at him that would have jolted a cow; and after
that she would sit and contemplate the corpse with
tranquil satisfaction — for she never missed her mosquito; she was a dead shot at short range. She
never removed a carcase, but left them there for bait.
I sat by this grim Sphynx and watched her till

thirty or forty mosquitoes — watched her, and waited
for her to say something, but she never did. So I
finally opened the conversation myself. I said:

"The mosquitoes are pretty bad, about here,
madam."

"You bet!"

"What did I understand you to say, madam?"

"YOU BET!"

Then she cheered up, and faced around and said:

"Danged if I didn't begin to think you fellers
was deef and dumb. I did, b' gosh. Here I've
sot, and sot, and sot, a-bust'n muskeeters and won-
derin' what was ailin' ye. Fust I thot you was deef
and dumb, then I thot you was sick or crazy, or
suthin', and then by and by I begin to reckon you
was a passel of sickly fools that couldn't think of
nothing to say. Wher'd ye come from?"

The Sphynx was a Sphynx no more! The fountains
of her great deep were broken up, and she rained
the nine parts of speech forty days and forty nights,
metaphorically speaking, and buried us under a deso-
lating deluge of trivial gossip that left not a crag
or pinnacle of rejoinder projecting above the tossing
waste of dislocated grammar and decomposed pro-
nunciation!

How we suffered, suffered, suffered! She went
on, hour after hour, till I was sorry I ever opened
the mosquito question and gave her a start. She
never did stop again until she got to her journey's
end toward daylight; and then she stirred us up as

she was leaving the stage (for we were nodding, by
that time), and said :

"Now you git out at Cottonwood, you fellers,
and lay over a couple o' days, and I'll be along some
time to-night, and if I can do ye any good by edgin'
in a word now and then, I'm right thar. Folks 'll
tell you 't I've always ben kind o' offish and partic'-
lar for a gal that's raised in the woods, and I *am*,
with the rag-tag and bob-tail, and a gal *has* to be,
if she wants to *be* anything, but when people comes
along which is my equals, I reckon I'm a pretty sociable heifer after all."

We resolved not to "lay by at Cottonwood."

CHAPTER III.

ABOUT an hour and a half before daylight we were bowling along smoothly over the road — so smoothly that our cradle only rocked in a gentle, lulling way, that was gradually soothing us to sleep, and dulling our consciousness — when something gave away under us! We were dimly aware of it, but indifferent to it. The coach stopped. We heard the driver and conductor talking together outside, and rummaging for a lantern, and swearing because they could not find it — but we had no interest in whatever had happened, and it only added to our comfort to think of those people out there at work in the murky night, and we snug in our nest with the curtains drawn. But presently, by the sounds, there seemed to be an examination going on, and then the driver's voice said:

" By George, the thoroughbrace is broke! "

This startled me broad awake — as an undefined sense of calamity is always apt to do. I said to myself: " Now, a thoroughbrace is probably part of a horse; and doubtless a vital part, too, from the dismay in the driver's voice. Leg, maybe — and yet how could he break his leg waltzing along such a

road as this? No, it can't be his leg. That is impossible, unless he was reaching for the driver.
Now, what can be the thoroughbrace of a horse, I
wonder? Well, whatever comes, I shall not air my
ignorance in this crowd, anyway.''

Just then the conductor's face appeared at a lifted
curtain, and his lantern glared in on us and our wall
of mail matter. He said:

"Gents, you'll have to turn out a spell!. Thoroughbrace is broke.''

We climbed out into a chill drizzle, and felt ever
so homeless and dreary. When I found that the
thing they called a '' thoroughbrace '' was the mas-
sive combination of belts and springs which the coach
rocks itself in, I said to the driver:

'' I never saw a thoroughbrace used up like that,
before, that I can remember. How did it happen?''

'' Why, it happened by trying to make one coach
carry three days' mail — that's how it happened,''
said he. "And right here is the very direction
which is wrote on all the newspaper-bags which was
to be put out for the Injuns for to keep 'em quiet.
It's most uncommon lucky, becuz it's so nation dark
I should 'a' gone by unbeknowns if that air thoroughbrace hadn't broke.''

I knew that he was in labor with another of those
winks of his, though I could not see his face, because he was bent down at work; and wishing him
a safe delivery, I turned to and helped the rest get
out the mail-sacks. It made a great pyramid by the

roadside when it was all out. When they had
mended the thoroughbrace we filled the two boots
again, but put no mail on top, and only half as much
inside as there was before. The conductor bent all
the seat backs down, and then filled the coach just
half full of mail-bags from end to end. We ob-
jected loudly to this, for it left us no seats. But the
conductor was wiser than we, and said a bed was
better than seats, and, moreover, this plan would pro-
tect his thoroughbraces. We never wanted any
seats after that. The lazy bed was infinitely prefer-
able. I had many an exciting day, subsequently,
lying on it reading the statutes and the dictionary,
and wondering how the characters would turn out.

The conductor said he would send back a guard
from the next station to take charge of the abandoned mail-bags, and we drove on.

It was now just dawn; and as we stretched our
cramped legs full length on the mail sacks, and
gazed out through the windows across the wide
wastes of greensward clad in cool, powdery mist, to
where there was an expectant look in the eastern
horizon, our perfect enjoyment took the form of a
tranquil and contented ecstasy. The stage whirled
along at a spanking gait, the breeze flapping curtains
and suspended coats in a most exhilarating way;
the cradle swayed and swung luxuriously, the pattering of the horses' hoofs, the cracking of the driver's
whip, and his " Hi-yi! g'lang! " were music; the
spinning ground and the waltzing trees appeared to

3

give us a mute hurrah as we went by, and then slack
up and look after us with interest, or envy, or something; and as we lay and smoked the pipe of peace
and compared all this luxury with the years of tiresome city life that had gone before it, we felt that
there was only one complete and satisfying happiness in the world, and we had found it.

After breakfast, at some station whose name I
have forgotten, we three climbed up on the seat
behind the driver, and let the conductor have our
bed for a nap.   And by and by, when the sun made
me drowsy, I lay down on my face on top of the
coach, grasping the slender iron railing, and slept for
an hour more.   That will give one an appreciable
idea of those matchless roads.   Instinct will make
a sleeping man grip a fast hold of the railing when
the stage jolts, but when it only swings and sways,
no grip is necessary.   Overland drivers and conductors used to sit in their places and sleep thirty or
forty minutes at a time, on good roads, while spinning along at the rate of eight or ten miles an hour.
I saw them do it, often.   There was no danger about
it; a sleeping man *will* seize the irons in time when
the coach jolts.   These men were hard worked, and it
was not possible for them to stay awake all the time.

By and by we passed through Marysville, and
over the Big Blue and Little Sandy; thence about a
mile, and entered Nebraska.   About a mile further
on, we came to the Big Sandy — one hundred and
eighty miles from St. Joseph.

As the sun was going down, we saw the first specimen of an animal known familiarly over two thousand miles of mountain and desert — from Kansas
clear to the Pacific Ocean — as the " jackass rabbit."
He is well named. He is just like any other rabbit,
except that he is from one-third to twice as large,
has longer legs in proportion to his size, and has the
most preposterous ears that ever were mounted on
any creature *but* a jackass. When he is sitting
quiet, thinking about his sins, or is absent-minded or
unapprehensive of danger, his majestic ears project
above him conspicuously; but the breaking of a twig
will scare him nearly to death, and then he tilts his
ears back gently and starts for home. All you can
see, then, for the next minute, is his long gray form
stretched out straight and " streaking it " through
the low sage-brush, head erect, eyes right, and ears
just canted a little to the rear, but showing you
where the animal is, all the time, the same as if he
carried a jib. Now and then he makes a marvelous
spring with his long legs, high over the stunted sage-
brush, and scores a leap that would make a horse
envious. Presently, he comes down to a long,
graceful " lope," and shortly he mysteriously disap-
pears. He has crouched behind a sage-bush, and
will sit there and listen and tremble until you get
within six feet of him, when he will get under way
again. But one must shoot at this creature once,
if he wishes to see him throw his heart into his
heels, and do the best he knows how. He is

frightened clear through, now, and he lays his long
ears down on his back, straightens himself out like
a yard-stick every spring he makes, and scatters
miles behind him with an easy indifference that is
enchanting.

Our party made this specimen "hump himself,"
as the conductor said. The Secretary started him
with a shot from the Colt; I commenced spitting at
him with my weapon; and all in the same instant the
old "Allen's" whole broadside let go with a rattling
crash, and it is not putting it too strong to say that
the rabbit was frantic! He dropped his ears, set up
his tail, and left for San Francisco at a speed which
can only be described as a flash and a vanish! Long
after he was out of sight we could hear him whiz.

I do not remember where we first came across
"sage-brush," but as I have been speaking of it I
may as well describe it. This is easily done, for if
the reader can imagine a gnarled and venerable live
oak tree reduced to a little shrub two feet high, with
its rough bark, its foliage, its twisted boughs, all
complete, he can picture the "sage-brush" exactly.
Often, on lazy afternoons in the mountains I have
lain on the ground with my face under a sage-bush,
and entertained myself with fancying that the gnats
among its foliage were lilliputian birds, and that the
ants marching and countermarching about its base
were lilliputian flocks and herds, and myself some
vast loafer from Brobdingnag waiting to catch a little
citizen and eat him.

It is an imposing monarch of the forest in ex-
quisite miniature, is the " sage-brush." Its foliage
is a grayish green, and gives that tint to desert and
mountain. It smells like our domestic sage, and
" sage-tea " made from it tastes like the sage-tea
which all boys are so well acquainted with. The
sage-brush is a singularly hardy plant, and grows
right in the midst of deep sand, and among barren
rocks, where nothing else in the vegetable world
would try to grow, except " bunch-grass."* The
sage-bushes grow from three to six or seven feet
apart, all over the mountains and deserts of the Far
West, clear to the borders of California. There is
not a tree of any kind in the deserts, for hundreds
of miles—there is no vegetation at all in a regular
desert, except the sage-brush and its cousin the
" greasewood," which is so much like the sage-brush
that the difference amounts to little. Camp-fires
and hot suppers in the deserts would be impossible
but for the friendly sage-brush. Its trunk is as large
as a boy's wrist (and from that up to a man's arm),
and its crooked branches are half as large as its
trunk—all good, sound, hard wood, very like oak.

When a party camps, the first thing to be done is

---

* " Bunch-grass " grows on the bleak mountain-sides of Nevada and
neighboring territories, and offers excellent feed for stock, even in the
dead of winter, wherever the snow is blown aside and exposes it ; notwithstanding its unpromising home, bunch-grass is a better and more
nutritious diet for cattle and horses than almost any other hay or grass
that is known — so stock-men say.

to cut sage-brush; and in a few minutes there is an opulent pile of it ready for use. A hole a foot wide, two feet deep, and two feet long, is dug, and sage-brush chopped up and burned in it till it is full to the brim with glowing coals; then the cooking begins, and there is no smoke, and consequently no swearing. Such a fire will keep all night, with very little replenishing; and it makes a very sociable camp-fire, and one around which the most impossible reminiscences sound plausible, instructive, and profoundly entertaining.

Sage-brush is very fair fuel, but as a vegetable it is a distinguished failure. Nothing can abide the taste of it but the jackass and his illegitimate child, the mule. But their testimony to its nutritiousness is worth nothing, for they will eat pine knots, or anthracite coal, or brass filings, or lead pipe, or old bottles, or anything that comes handy, and then go off looking as grateful as if they had had oysters for dinner. Mules and donkeys and camels have appetites that anything will relieve temporarily, but nothing satisfy. In Syria, once, at the head-waters of the Jordan, a camel took charge of my overcoat while the tents were being pitched, and examined it with a critical eye, all over, with as much interest as if he had an idea of getting one made like it; and then, after he was done figuring on it as an article of apparel, he began to contemplate it as an article of diet. He put his foot on it, and lifted one of the sleeves out with his teeth, and chewed and chewed

at it, gradually taking it in, and all the while opening and closing his eyes in a kind of religious
ecstasy, as if he had never tasted anything as good
as an overcoat before in his life. Then he smacked
his lips once or twice, and reached after the other
sleeve. Next he tried the velvet collar, and smiled
a smile of such contentment that it was plain to see
that he regarded that as the daintiest thing about an
overcoat. The tails went next, along with some per-
cussion caps and cough candy, and some fig-paste
from Constantinople. And then my newspaper correspondence dropped out, and he took a chance in
that — manuscript letters written for the home
papers. But he was treading on dangerous ground,
now. He began to come across solid wisdom in
those documents that was rather weighty on his
stomach; and occasionally he would take a joke
that would shake him up till it loosened his teeth;
it was getting to be perilous times with him, but he
held his grip with good courage and hopefully, till
at last he began to stumble on statements that not
even a camel could swallow with impunity. He began to gag and gasp, and his eyes to stand out, and
his forelegs to spread, and in about a quarter of a
minute he fell over as stiff as a carpenter's work-
bench, and died a death of indescribable agony. I
went and pulled the manuscript out of his mouth,
and found that the sensitive creature had choked to
death on one of the mildest and gentlest statements
of fact that I ever laid before a trusting public.

3*

I was about to say, when diverted from my subject, that occasionally one finds sage-bushes five or six feet high, and with a spread of branch and foliage in proportion, but two or two and a half feet is the usual height.

CHAPTER IV.

AS the sun went down and the evening chill came
on, we made preparation for bed. We stirred
up the hard leather letter-sacks, and the knotty
canvas bags of printed matter (knotty and uneven
because of projecting ends and corners of magazines,
boxes and books). We stirred them up and redis-
posed them in such a way as to make our bed as
level as possible. And we *did* improve it, too,
though after all our work it had an upheaved and
billowy look about it, like a little piece of a stormy
sea. Next we hunted up our boots from odd nooks
among the mail bags where they had settled, and
put them on. Then we got down our coats, vests,
pantaloons and heavy woolen shirts, from the arm-
loops where they had been swinging all day, and
clothed ourselves in them — for, there being no
ladies either at the stations or in the coach, and the
weather being hot, we had looked to our comfort by
stripping to our underclothing, at nine o'clock in
the morning. All things being now ready, we
stowed the uneasy Dictionary where it would lie as
quiet as possible, and placed the water-canteen and

C*   (35)

pistols where we could find them in the dark.   Then
we smoked a final pipe, and swapped a final yarn;
after which, we put the pipes, tobacco, and bag of
coin in snug holes and caves among the mail-bags,
and then fastened down the coach curtains all around
and made the place as "dark as the inside of a cow,"
as the conductor phrased it in his picturesque way.
It was certainly as dark as any place could be —
nothing was even dimly visible in it.   And finally,
we rolled ourselves up like silk-worms, each person
in his own blanket, and sank peacefully to sleep.

Whenever the stage stopped to change horses, we
would wake up, and try to recollect where we were
— and succeed — and in a minute or two the stage
would be off again, and we likewise.   We began to
get into country, now, threaded here and there with
little streams.   These had high, steep banks on each
side, and every time we flew down one bank and
scrambled up the other, our party inside got mixed
somewhat.   First we would all be down in a pile at
the forward end of the stage, nearly in a sitting posture, and in a second we would shoot to the other
end, and stand on our heads.   And we would sprawl
and kick, too, and ward off ends and corners of mail-
bags that came lumbering over us and about us; and
as the dust rose from the tumult, we would all sneeze
in chorus, and the majority of us would grumble,
and probably say some hasty thing, like: "Take
your elbow out of my ribs! — can't you quit
crowding?"

Every time we avalanched from one end of the stage to the other, the Unabridged Dictionary would come too; and every time it came it damaged somebody. One trip it " barked " the Secretary's elbow; the next trip it hurt me in the stomach, and the third it tilted Bemis's nose up till he could look down his nostrils — he said. The pistols and coin soon settled to the bottom, but the pipes, pipe-stems, tobacco, and canteens clattered and floundered after the Dictionary every time it made an assault on us, and aided and abetted the book by spilling tobacco in our eyes, and water down our backs.

Still, all things considered, it was a very comfortable night. It wore gradually away, and when at last a cold gray light was visible through the puckers and chinks in the curtains, we yawned and stretched with satisfaction, shed our cocoons, and felt that we had slept as much as was necessary. By and by, as the sun rose up and warmed the world, we pulled off our clothes and got ready for breakfast. We were just pleasantly in time, for five minutes afterward the driver sent the weird music of his bugle winding over the grassy solitudes, and presently we detected a low hut or two in the distance. Then the rattling of the coach, the clatter of our six horses' hoofs, and the driver's crisp commands, awoke to a louder and stronger emphasis, and we went sweeping down on the station at our smartest speed. It was fascinating — that old Overland stage-coaching.

We jumped out in undress uniform. The driver

tossed his gathered reins out on the ground, gaped
and stretched complacently, drew off his heavy
buckskin gloves with great deliberation and insuffer-
able dignity — taking not the slightest notice of a
dozen solicitous inquiries after his health, and humbly
facetious and flattering accostings, and obsequious
tenders of service, from five or six hairy and half-
civilized station-keepers and hostlers who were nimbly
unhitching our steeds and bringing the fresh team
out of the stables — for, in the eyes of the stage-driver
of that day, station-keepers and hostlers were a sort
of good enough low creatures, useful in their place,
and helping to make up a world, but not the kind of
beings which a person of distinction could afford to
concern himself with; while, on the contrary, in the
eyes of the station-keeper and the hostler, the stage-
driver was a hero — a great and shining dignitary, the
world's favorite son, the envy of the people, the observed of the nations. When they spoke to him
they received his insolent silence meekly, and as
being the natural and proper conduct of so great a
man; when he opened his lips they all hung on his
words with admiration (he never honored a particular individual with a remark, but addressed it with a
broad generality to the horses, the stables, the surrounding country *and* the human underlings);
when he discharged a facetious insulting personality
at a hostler, that hostler was happy for the day;
when he uttered his one jest — old as the hills, coarse,
profane, witless, and inflicted on the same audience,

in the same language, every time his coach drove up there — the varlets roared, and slapped their thighs, and swore it was the best thing they'd ever heard in all their lives. And how they would fly around when he wanted a basin of water, a gourd of the same, or a light for his pipe! — but they would instantly insult a passenger if he so far forgot himself as to crave a favor at their hands. They could do that sort of insolence as well as the driver they copied it from — for, let it be borne in mind, the Overland driver had but little less contempt for his passengers than he had for his hostlers.

The hostlers and station-keepers treated the really powerful *conductor* of the coach merely with the best of what was their idea of civility, but the *driver* was the only being they bowed down to and worshiped. How admiringly they would gaze up at him in his high seat as he gloved himself with lingering delib- eration, while some happy hostler held the bunch of reins aloft, and waited patiently for him to take it! And how they would bombard him with glorifying ejaculations as he cracked his long whip and went careering away.

The station buildings were long, low huts, made of sun-dried, mud-colored bricks, laid up without mortar (*adobes*, the Spaniards call these bricks, and Americans shorten it to *'dobies*). The roofs, which had no slant to them worth speaking of, were thatched and then sodded or covered with a thick layer of earth, and from this sprung a pretty rank growth of

weeds and grass. It was the first time we had ever
seen a man's front yard on top of his house. The
buildings consisted cf barns, stable-room for twelve
or fifteen horses, and a hut for an eating-room for
passengers. This latter had bunks in it for the station-keeper and a hostler or two. You could rest
your elbow on its eaves, and you had to bend in order
to get in at the door. In place of a window there
was a square hole about large enough for a man to
crawl through, but this had no glass in it. There
was no flooring, but the ground was packed hard.
There was no stove, but the fireplace served all
needful purposes. There were no shelves, no cup-
boards, no closets. In a corner stood an open sack
of flour, and nestling against its base were a couple
of black and venerable tin coffee-pots, a tin teapot, a
little bag of salt, and a side of bacon.

By the door of the station-keeper's den, outside,
was a tin wash-basin, on the ground. Near it was a
pail of water and a piece of yellow bar soap, and
from the eaves hung a hoary blue woolen shirt, sig-
nificantly — but this latter was the station-keeper's
private towel, and only two persons in all the party
might venture to use it — the stage-driver and the
conductor. The latter would not, from a sense of
decency; the former would not, because he did not
choose to encourage the advances of a station-keeper.
We had towels — in the valise; they might as well
have been in Sodom and Gomorrah. We (and the
conductor) used our handkerchiefs, and the driver

his pantaloons and sleeves.   By the door, inside, was
fastened a small old-fashioned looking-glass frame,
with two little fragments of the original mirror
lodged down in one corner of it.   This arrangement
afforded a pleasant double-barreled portrait of you
when you looked into it, with one-half of your head
set up a couple of inches above the other half.   From
the glass frame hung the half of a comb by a string
— but if I had to describe that patriarch or die, I
believe I would order some sample coffins.   It had
come down from Esau and Samson, and had been
accumulating hair ever since — along with certain im-
purities.   In one corner of the room stood three or
four rifles and muskets, together with horns and
pouches of ammunition.   The station-men wore
pantaloons of coarse, country-woven stuff, and into
the seat and the inside of the legs were sewed ample
additions of buckskin, to do duty in place of leg-
gings, when the man rode horseback — so the pants
were half dull blue and half yellow, and unspeakably
picturesque.   The pants were stuffed into the tops
of high boots, the heels whereof were armed with
great Spanish spurs, whose little iron clogs and
chains jingled with every step.   The man wore a
huge beard and mustachios, an old slouch hat, a
blue woolen shirt, no suspenders, no vest, no coat
— in a leathern sheath in his belt, a great long
" navy " revolver (slung on right side, hammer to
the front), and projecting from his boot a horn-
handled bowie-knife.   The furniture of the hut was

neither gorgeous nor much in the way. The rock-
ing-chairs and sofas were not present, and never had
been, but they were represented by two three-legged
stools, a pineboard bench four feet long, and two
empty candle-boxes. The table was a greasy board
on stilts, and the table-cloth and napkins had not
come — and they were not looking for them, either.
A battered tin platter, a knife and fork, and a tin
pint cup, were at each man's place, and the driver
had a queens-ware saucer that had seen better days.
Of course, this duke sat at the head of the table.
There was one isolated piece of table furniture that
bore about it a touching air of grandeur in misfortune. This was the caster. It was German silver,
and crippled and rusty, but it was so preposterously
out of place there that it was suggestive of a tattered
exiled king among barbarians, and the majesty of its
native position compelled respect even in its degradation. There was only one cruet left, and that was
a stopperless, fly-specked, broken-necked thing, with
two inches of vinegar in it, and a dozen preserved
flies with their heels up and looking sorry they had
invested there.

The station-keeper up-ended a disk of last week's
bread, of the shape and size of an old-time cheese,
and carved some slabs from it which were as good as
Nicholson pavement, and tenderer.

He sliced off a piece of bacon for each man, but
only the experienced old hands made out to eat it,
for it was condemned army bacon which the United

States would not feed to its soldiers in the forts, and
the stage company had bought it cheap for the sus-
tenance of their passengers and employés.   We may
have found this condemned army bacon further out
on the plains than the section I am locating it in, but
we *found* it — there is no gainsaying that.

Then he poured for us a beverage which he called
" *Slumgullion*," and it is hard to think he was not
inspired when he named it.   It really pretended to
be tea, but there was too much dish-rag, and sand,
and old bacon-rind in it to deceive the intelligent
traveler.   He had no sugar and no milk — not even
a spoon to stir the ingredients with.

We could not eat the bread or the meat, nor drink
the "slumgullion."   And when I looked at that
melancholy vinegar-cruet, I thought of the anecdote
(a very, very old one, even at that day) of the traveler who sat down to a table which had nothing on it
but a mackerel and a pot of mustard.   He asked the
landlord if this was all.   The landlord said:

" *All!*   Why, thunder and lightning, I should
think there was mackerel enough there for six."

" But I don't like mackerel."

" Oh — then help yourself to the mustard."

In other days I had considered it a good, a very
good, anecdote, but there was a dismal plausibility
about it, here, that took all the humor out of it.

Our breakfast was before us, but our teeth were
idle.

I tasted and smelt, and said I would take coffee, I
4

believed. The station-boss stopped dead still, and glared at me speechless. At last, when he came to, he turned away and said, as one who communes with himself upon a matter too vast to grasp:

"Coffee! Well, if that don't go clean ahead of me, I'm d—d!"

We could not eat, and there was no conversation among the hostlers and herdsmen — we all sat at the same board. At least there was no conversation further than a single hurried request, now and then, from one employé to another. It was always in the same form, and always gruffly friendly. Its western freshness and novelty startled me, at first, and interested me; but it presently grew monotonous, and lost its charm. It was:

" Pass the bread, you son of a skunk!" No, I forget— skunk was not the word; it seems to me it was still stronger than that; I know it was, in fact, but it is gone from my memory, apparently. However, it is no matter — probably it was too strong for print, anyway. It is the landmark in my memory which tells me where I first encountered the vigorous new vernacular of the occidental plains and mountains.

We gave up the breakfast, and paid our dollar apiece and went back to our mail-bag bed in the coach, and found comfort in our pipes. Right here we suffered the first diminution of our princely state. We left our six fine horses and took six mules in their place. But they were wild Mexican fellows, and a man had to stand at the head of each of them and hold him fast while the driver gloved and got himself ready. And when at last he grasped the reins and gave the word, the men sprung suddenly away from the mules' heads and the coach shot from the station as if it had issued from a cannon. How the frantic animals did scamper! It was a fierce and furious gallop — and the gait never altered for a moment till we reeled off ten or twelve miles and swept up to the next collection of little station-huts and stables.

So we flew along all day. At 2 P. M. the belt of timber that fringes the North Platte and marks its windings through the vast level floor of the Plains came in sight. At 4 P. M. we crossed a branch of the river, and at 5 P. M. we crossed the Platte itself, and landed at Fort Kearney, *fifty-six hours out from St. Joe* — THREE HUNDRED MILES!

Now that was stage-coaching on the great Overland, ten or twelve years ago, when perhaps not more than ten men in America, all told, expected to live to see a railroad follow that route to the Pacific. But the railroad is there, now, and it pictures a thousand odd comparisons and contrasts in my mind to read the following sketch, in the New York *Times*, of a recent trip over almost the very ground I have been describing. I can scarcely comprehend the new state of things:

"ACROSS THE CONTINENT.

"At 4.20 P.M., Sunday, we rolled out of the station at Omaha, and started westward on our long jaunt. A couple of hours out, dinner was announced—an 'event' to those of us who had yet to experience what it is to eat in one of Pullman's hotels on wheels; so, stepping into the car next forward of our sleeping palace, we found ourselves in the dining-car. It was a revelation to us, that first dinner on Sunday. And though we continued to dine for four days, and had as many breakfasts and suppers, our whole party never ceased to admire the perfection of the arrangements, and the marvelous results achieved. Upon tables covered with snowy linen, and garnished with services of solid silver, Ethiop waiters, flitting about in spotless white, placed as by magic a repast at which Delmonico himself could have had no occasion to blush; and, indeed, in some respects it would be hard for that distinguished *chef* to match our *menu ;* for, in addition to all that ordinarily makes up a first-chop dinner, had we not our antelope steak (the gormand who has not experienced this — bah! what does he know of the feast of fat things ?) our delicious mountain-brook trout, and choice fruits and berries, and (sauce piquant and unpurchasable!) our sweet-scented, appetite-compelling air of the prairies ? You may depend upon it, we all did justice to the good things, and as we washed them down with bumpers of sparkling Krug, whilst we sped along at the rate of thirty miles an hour, agreed it was the *fastest* living we had ever experienced. (We beat that, however, two days afterward when we made *twenty-seven miles in twenty-seven minutes*, while our Champagne glasses filled to the brim spilled not a drop!) After dinner we repaired to our drawing-room car, and, as it was Sabbath eve, intoned some of the grand old hymns — 'Praise God from whom,' etc.; 'Shining Shore,' 'Coronation,' etc. — the voices of the men singers and of the women singers blending sweetly in the evening air, while our train, with its great, glaring Polyphemus eye, lighting up long vistas of prairie, rushed into the night and the Wild. Then to bed in luxurious couches, where we slept the sleep of the just and only awoke the next morning (Monday) at eight o'clock, to find ourselves at the crossing of the North Platte, three hundred miles from Omaha — *fifteen hours and forty minutes out.*"

CHAPTER V.

ANOTHER night of alternate tranquillity and turmoil. But morning came, by and by. It was another glad awakening to fresh breezes, vast expanses of level greensward, bright sunlight, an impressive solitude utterly without visible human beings or human habitations, and an atmosphere of such amazing magnifying properties that trees that seemed close at hand were more than three miles away. We resumed undress uniform, climbed a-top of the flying coach, dangled our legs over the side, shouted occasionally at our frantic mules, merely to see them lay their ears back and scamper faster, tied our hats on to keep our hair from blowing away, and leveled an outlook over the world-wide carpet about us for things new and strange to gaze at. Even at this day it thrills me through and through to think of the life, the gladness and the wild sense of freedom that used to make the blood dance in my veins on those fine overland mornings!

Along about an hour after breakfast we saw the first prairie-dog villages, the first antelope, and the first wolf. If I remember rightly, this latter was the

regular *cayote* (pronounced ky-*o*-te) of the farther
deserts. And if it *was*, he was not a pretty creature,
or respectable either, for I got well acquainted with
his race afterward, and can speak with confidence.
The cayote is a long, slim, sick and sorry-looking
skeleton, with a gray wolf-skin stretched over it, a
tolerably bushy tail that forever sags down with a
despairing expression of forsakenness and misery,
a furtive and evil eye, and a long, sharp face, with
slightly lifted lip and exposed teeth. He has a
general slinking expression all over. The cayote
is a living, breathing allegory of Want. He is
always hungry. He is always poor, out of luck and
friendless. The meanest creatures despise him, and
even the fleas would desert him for a velocipede.
He is so spiritless and cowardly that even while his
exposed teeth are pretending a threat, the rest of his
face is apologizing for it. And he is *so* homely! — so
scrawny, and ribby, and coarse-haired, and pitiful.
When he sees you he lifts his lip and lets a flash of
his teeth out, and then turns a little out of the course
he was pursuing, depresses his head a bit, and strikes
a long, soft-footed trot through the sage-brush,
glancing over his shoulder at you, from time to time,
till he is about out of easy pistol range, and then he
stops and takes a deliberate survey of you; he will
trot fifty yards and stop again — another fifty and
stop again; and finally the gray of his gliding body
blends with the gray of the sage-brush, and he dis-
appears. All this is when you make no demonstra-

tion against him; but if you do, he develops a live-
lier interest in his journey, and instantly electrifies
his heels and puts such a deal of real estate between
himself and your weapon, that by the time you have
raised the hammer you see that you need a minie
rifle, and by the time you have got him in line you
need a rifled cannon, and by the time you have
" drawn a bead " on him you see well enough that
nothing but an unusually long-winded streak of lightning could reach him where he is now. But if you
start a swift-footed dog after him, you will enjoy it
ever so much — especially if it is a dog that has a
good opinion of himself, and has been brought up
to think he knows something about speed. The
cayote will go swinging gently off on that deceitful
trot of his, and every little while he will smile a
fraudful smile over his shoulder that will fill that
dog entirely full of encouragement and worldly ambition, and make him lay his head still lower to the
ground, and stretch his neck further to the front, and
pant more fiercely, and stick his tail out straighter
behind, and move his furious legs with a yet wilder
frenzy, and leave a broader and broader, and higher
and denser cloud of desert sand smoking behind, and
marking his long wake across the level plain ! And
all this time the dog is only a short twenty feet behind the cayote, and to save the soul of him he cannot understand why it is that he cannot get percep-
tibly closer; and he begins to get aggravated, and it
makes him madder and madder to see how gently

4.

the cayote glides along and never pants or sweats or ceases to smile; and he grows still more and more incensed to see how shamefully he has been taken in by an entire stranger, and what an ignoble swindle that long, calm, soft-footed trot is; and next he notices that he is getting fagged, and that the cayote actually has to slacken speed a little to keep from running away from him — and *then* that town-dog is mad in earnest, and he begins to strain and weep and swear, and paw the sand higher than ever, and reach for the cayote with concentrated and desperate energy. This "spurt" finds him six feet behind the gliding enemy, and two miles from his friends. And then, in the instant that a wild new hope is lighting up his face, the cayote turns and smiles blandly upon him once more, and with a something about it which seems to say: "Well, I shall have to tear myself away from you, bub — business is business, and it will not do for me to be fooling along this way all day"— and forthwith there is a rushing sound, and the sudden splitting of a long crack through the atmosphere, and behold that dog is solitary and alone in the midst of a vast solitude!

It makes his head swim. He stops, and looks all around; climbs the nearest sand-mound, and gazes into the distance; shakes his head reflectively, and then, without a word, he turns and jogs along back to his train, and takes up a humble position under the hindmost wagon, and feels unspeakably mean, and looks ashamed, and hangs his tail at half-mast

for a week. And for as much as a year after that,
whenever there is a great hue and cry after a
cayote, that dog will merely glance in that direction
without emotion, and apparently observe to himself,
" I believe I do not wish any of the pie."

The cayote lives chiefly in the most desolate and
forbidding deserts, along with the lizard, the jackass-
rabbit and the raven, and gets an uncertain and precarious living, and earns it. He seems to subsist
almost wholly on the carcasses of oxen, mules, and
horses that have dropped out of emigrant trains and
died, and upon windfalls of carrion, and occasional
legacies of offal bequeathed to him by white men
who have been opulent enough to have something
better to butcher than condemned army bacon. He
will eat anything in the world that his first cousins,
the desert-frequenting tribes of Indians, will, and they
will eat anything they can bite. It is a curious fact
that these latter are the only creatures known to history who will eat nitro-glycerine and ask for more if
they survive.

The cayote of the deserts beyond the Rocky
Mountains has a peculiarly hard time of it, owing to
the fact that his relations, the Indians, are just as apt
to be the first to detect a seductive scent on the des
ert breeze, and follow the fragrance to the late ox it
emanated from, as he is himself; and when this oc ·
curs he has to content himself with sitting off at a
little distance watching those people strip off and dig
out everything edible, and walk off with it. Then

D*

he and the waiting ravens explore the skeleton and polish the bones. It is considered that the cayote, and the obscene bird, and the Indian of the desert, testify their blood kinship with each other in that they live together in the waste places of the earth on terms of perfect confidence and friendship, while hating all other creatures and yearning to assist at their funerals. He does not mind going a hundred miles to breakfast, and a hundred and fifty to dinner, because he is sure to have three or four days between meals, and he can just as well be traveling and looking at the scenery as lying around doing nothing and adding to the burdens of his parents.

We soon learned to recognize the sharp, vicious bark of the cayote as it came across the murky plain at night to disturb our dreams among the mail-sacks; and remembering his forlorn aspect and his hard fortune, made shift to wish him the blessed novelty of a long day's good luck and a limitless larder the morrow.

CHAPTER VI.

OUR new conductor (just shipped) had been without sleep for twenty hours. Such a thing was very frequent. From St. Joseph, Missouri, to Sacramento, California, by stage-coach, was nearly nineteen hundred miles, and the trip was often made in fifteen days (the cars do it in four and a half, now), but the time specified in the mail contracts, and required by the schedule, was eighteen or nineteen days, if I remember rightly. This was to make fair allowance for winter storms and snows, and other unavoidable causes of detention. The stage company had everything under strict discipline and good system. Over each two hundred and fifty miles of road they placed an agent or superintendent, and invested him with great authority. His beat or jurisdiction of two hundred and fifty miles was called a "division." He purchased horses, mules, harness, and food for men and beasts, and distributed these things among his stage stations, from time to time, according to his judgment of what each station needed. He erected station buildings and dug wells. He attended to the paying of the station-keepers, hostlers, drivers, and blacksmiths, and discharged them whenever he chose. He was a very, very great man in his " division " — a kind of Grand Mogul, a Sultan of the Indies, in whose presence common men were modest of speech and manner, and in the glare of whose greatness even the dazzling stage-driver dwindled to a penny dip. There were about eight of these kings, all told, on the Overland route.

Next in rank and importance to the division-agent came the " conductor." His beat was the same length as the agent's — two hundred and fifty miles. He sat with the driver, and (when necessary) rode that fearful distance, night and day, without other rest or sleep than what he could get perched thus on top of the flying vehicle. Think of it! He had absolute charge of the mails, express matter, passengers, and stage-coach, until he delivered them to the next conductor, and got his receipt for them. Consequently he had to be a man of intelligence, decision, and considerable executive ability. He was usually a quiet, pleasant man, who attended closely to his duties, and was a good deal of a gentleman. It was not absolutely necessary that the division-agent should be a gentleman, and occasionally he wasn't. But he was always a general in administrative ability, and a bull-dog in courage and determination — otherwise the chieftainship over the lawless underlings of the Overland service would never in any instance have been to him anything but an equivalent for a month of insolence and distress and a bullet and a coffin at the end of it. There were about sixteen or eighteen conductors on the Overland, for there was a daily stage each way, and a conductor on every stage.

Next in *real* and official rank and importance, *after* the conductor, came my delight, the driver — next in real but not in *apparent* importance — for we have seen that in the eyes of the common herd the driver was to the conductor as an admiral is to the captain of the flag-ship. The driver's beat was pretty long, and his sleeping-time at the stations pretty short, sometimes; and so, but for the grandeur of his position his would have been a sorry life, as well as a hard and a wearing one. We took a new driver every day or every night (for they drove backward and forward over the same piece of road all the time), and therefore we never got as well acquainted with them as we did with the conductors; and besides, they would have been above being familiar with such rubbish as passengers, anyhow, as a general thing. Still, we were always eager to get a sight of each and every new driver as soon as the watch changed, for each and every day we were either anxious to get rid of an unpleasant one, or loath to part with a driver we had learned to like and had come to be sociable and friendly with. And so the first question we asked the conductor whenever we got to where we were to exchange drivers, was always, " Which is him? " The grammar was faulty, maybe, but we could not know, then, that it would go into a book some day. As long as everything went smoothly, the Overland driver was well enough situated, but if a fellow driver got sick suddenly it made trouble, for the coach *must* go on, and so the potentate who was about to climb down and take a luxurious rest after his long night's siege in the midst of wind and rain and darkness, had to stay where he was and do the sick man's work. Once in the Rocky Mountains, when I found a driver sound asleep on the box, and the mules going at the usual break-neck pace, the conductor said never mind him, there was no danger, and he was doing double duty — had driven seventy-five miles on one coach, and was now going back over it on this without rest or sleep. A hundred and fifty miles of holding back of six vindictive mules and keeping them from climbing the trees! It sounds incredible, but I remember the statement well enough.

The station-keepers, hostlers, etc., were low, rough characters, as already described; and from western Nebraska to Nevada a considerable sprinkling of them might be fairly set down as outlaws — fugitives from justice, criminals whose best security was a section of country which was without law and without even the pretense of it. When the " division-agent " issued an order to one of these parties he did it with the full understanding that he might have to enforce it with a navy six-shooter, and so he always went " fixed " to make things go along smoothly. Now

and then a division-agent was really obliged to shoot
a hostler through the head to teach him some simple
matter that he could have taught him with a club if
his circumstances and surroundings had been different. But they were snappy, able men, those divis-
ion-agents, and when they tried to teach a subordinate anything, that subordinate generally " got it
through his head."

A great portion of this vast machinery — these
hundreds of men and coaches, and thousands of mules
and horses — was in the hands of Mr. Ben Holliday.
All the western half of the business was in his
hands. This reminds me of an incident of Palestine
travel which is pertinent here, and so I will transfer
it just in the language in which I find it set down in
my Holy Land note-book:

No doubt everybody has heard of Ben Holliday — a man of prodigious energy, who used to send mails and passengers flying across the
continent in his overland stage-coaches like a very whirlwind — two
thousand long miles in fifteen days and a half, by the watch! But this
fragment of history is not about Ben Holliday, but about a young New
York boy by the name of Jack, who traveled with our small party of
pilgrims in the Holy Land (and who had traveled to California in Mr.
Holliday's overland coaches three years before, and had by no means
forgotton it or lost his gushing admiration of Mr. H.). Aged nineteen.
Jack was a good boy — a good-hearted and always well-meaning boy,
who had been reared in the city of New York, and although he was
bright and knew a great many useful things, his Scriptural education
had been a good deal neglected — to such a degree, indeed, that all
Holy Land history was fresh and new to him, and all Bible names mys-
teries that had never disturbed his virgin ear. Also in our party was an
elderly pilgrim who was the reverse of Jack, in that he was learned in
the Scriptures and an enthusiast concerning them. He was our ency-
clopedia, and we were never tired of listening to his speeches, nor he of

making them. He never passed a celebrated locality, from Bashan to Bethlehem, without illuminating it with an oration. One day, when camped near the ruins of Jericho, he burst forth with something like this :

"Jack, do you see that range of mountains over yonder that bounds the Jordan valley ? The mountains of Moab, Jack ! Think of it, my boy — the actual mountains of Moab — renowned in Scripture history ! We are actually standing face to face with those illustrious crags and peaks — and for all we know " [dropping his voice impressively], *our eyes may be resting at this very moment upon the spot* WHERE LIES THE MYSTERIOUS GRAVE OF MOSES ! Think of it, Jack ! "

"Moses *who ?* " (falling inflection).

"Moses *who !* Jack, you ought to be ashamed of yourself — you ought to be ashamed of such criminal ignorance. Why, Moses, the great guide, soldier, poet, lawgiver of ancient Israel ! Jack, from this spot where we stand, to Egypt, stretches a fearful desert three hundred miles in extent — and across that desert that wonderful man brought the children of Israel ! — guiding them with unfailing sagacity for forty years over the sandy desolation and among the obstructing rocks and hills, and landed them at last, safe and sound, within sight of this very spot; and where we now stand they entered the Promised Land with anthems of rejoicing ! It was a wonderful, wonderful thing to do, Jack ! Think of it ! "

"*Forty years ? Only three hundred miles ?* Humph ! Ben Holliday would have fetched them through in thirty-six hours ! "

The boy meant no harm. He did not know that he had said anything that was wrong or irreverent. And so no one scolded him or felt offended with him — and nobody *could* but some ungenerous spirit incapable of excusing the heedless blunders of a boy.

At noon on the fifth day out, we arrived at the "Crossing of the South Platte," *alias* "Julesburg," *alias* " Overland City," four hundred and seventy miles from St. Joseph — the strangest, quaintest, funniest frontier town that our untraveled eyes had ever stared at and been astonished with.

CHAPTER VII.

IT did seem strange enough to see a town again after what appeared to us such a long acquaintance with deep, still, almost lifeless and houseless solitude! We tumbled out into the busy street feeling like meteoric people crumbled off the corner of some other world, and wakened up suddenly in this. For an hour we took as much interest in Overland City as if we had never seen a town before. The reason we had an hour to spare was because we had to change our stage (for a less sumptuous affair, called a " mud-wagon ") and transfer our freight of mails.

Presently we got under way again. We came to the shallow, yellow, muddy South Platte, with its low banks and its scattering flat sand-bars and pigmy islands — a melancholy stream straggling through the center of the enormous flat plain, and only saved from being impossible to find with the naked eye by its sentinel rank of scattering trees standing on either bank. The Platte was " up," they said — which made me wish I could see it when it was down, if it could look any sicker and sorrier. They said it was

5

a dangerous stream to cross, now, because its quick-sands were liable to swallow up horses, coach, and passengers if an attempt was made to ford it. But the mails had to go, and we made the attempt. Once or twice in midstream the wheels sunk into the yielding sands so threateningly that we half believed we had dreaded and avoided the sea all our lives to be shipwrecked in a " mud-wagon " in the middle of a desert at last. But we dragged through and sped away toward the setting sun.

Next morning just before dawn, when about five hundred and fifty miles from St. Joseph, our mud-wagon broke down. We were to be delayed five or six hours, and therefore we took horses, by invita-tion, and joined a party who were just starting on a buffalo hunt. It was noble sport galloping over the plain in the dewy freshness of the morning, but our part of the hunt ended in disaster and disgrace, for a wounded buffalo bull chased the passenger Bemis nearly two miles, and then he forsook his horse and took to a lone tree. He was very sullen about the matter for some twenty-four hours, but at last he began to soften little by little, and finally he said:

" Well, it was not funny, and there was no sense in those gawks making themselves so facetious over it. I tell you I was angry in earnest for awhile. I should have shot that long gangly lubber they called Hank, if I could have done it without crippling six or seven other people — but of course I couldn't, the old 'Allen' 's so confounded comprehensive. I wish those loafers had been up in the tree; they wouldn't have wanted to laugh so. If I had had a horse worth a cent—but no, the minute he saw that buffalo bull wheel on him and give a bellow, he raised straight up in the air and stood on his heels. The saddle began to slip, and I took him round the neck and laid close to him, and began to pray. Then he came down and stood up on the other end awhile, and the bull actually stopped pawing sand and bellowing to contemplate the inhuman spectacle. Then the bull made a pass at him and uttered a bellow that sounded perfectly frightful, it was so close to me, and that seemed to literally prostrate my horse's reason, and make a raving distracted maniac of him, and I wish I may die if he didn't stand on his head for a quarter of a minute and shed tears. He was absolutely out of his mind—he was, as sure as truth itself, and he really didn't know what he was doing. Then the bull came charging at us, and my horse dropped down on all fours and took a fresh start— and then for the next ten minutes he would actually throw one handspring after another so fast that the bull began to get unsettled, too, and didn't know where to start in—and so he stood there sneezing, and shoveling dust over his back, and bellowing every now and then, and thinking he had got a fifteen-hundred dollar circus horse for breakfast, certain. Well, I was first out on his neck—the horse's, not the bull's—and then underneath, and next on his rump, and sometimes head up, and sometimes heels — but I tell you it seemed solemn and awful to be ripping and tearing and carrying on so in the presence of death, as you might say. Pretty soon the bull made a snatch for us and brought away some of my horse's tail (I suppose, but do not know, being pretty busy at the time), but *something* made him hungry for solitude and suggested to him to get up and hunt for it. And then you ought to have seen that spider-legged old skeleton go! and you ought to have seen the bull cut out after him, too — head down, tongue out, tail up, bellowing like everything, and actually mowing down the weeds, and tearing up the earth, and boosting up the sand like a whirlwind! By George, it was a hot race! I and the saddle were back on the rump, and I had the bridle in my teeth and holding on to the pommel with both hands. First we left the dogs behind; then we passed a jackass rabbit; then we overtook a cayote, and were gaining on an antelope when the rotten girths let go and threw me about thirty yards off to the left, and as the saddle went down over the horse's rump he gave it a lift with his heels that sent it more than four hundred yards up in the air, I wish I may die in a minute if he didn't. I fell at the foot of the only solitary tree there was in nine counties adjacent (as any creature could see with the naked eye), and the next second I had hold of the bark with four sets of nails and my teeth, and the next second after that I was astraddle of the main limb and blaspheming my luck in a way that

made my breath smell of brimstone. I *had* the bull,
now, if he did not think of *one* thing. But that one
thing I dreaded. I dreaded it very seriously. There
was a possibility that the bull might not think of it,
but there were greater chances that he would. I
made up my mind what I would do in case he did.
It was a little over forty feet to the ground from
where I sat. I cautiously unwound the lariat from
the pommel of my saddle—"

"Your *saddle?* Did you take your saddle up in
the tree with you?"

"Take it up in the tree with me? Why, how you
talk. Of course I didn't. No man could do that.
It *fell* in the tree when it came down."

"Oh — exactly."

"Certainly. I unwound the lariat, and fastened
one end of it to the limb. It was the very best
green raw-hide, and capable of sustaining tons. I
made a slip-noose in the other end, and then hung
it down to see the length. It reached down twenty-
two feet — half way to the ground. I then loaded
every barrel of the Allen with a double charge. I
felt satisfied. I said to myself, if he never thinks of
that one thing that I dread, all right — but if he does,
all right anyhow — I am fixed for him. But don't
you know that the very thing a man dreads is the
thing that always happens? Indeed it is so. I
watched the bull, now, with anxiety — anxiety which
no one can conceive of who has not been in such a
situation and felt that at any moment death might

come. Presently a thought came into the bull's
eye. I knew it! said I — if my nerve fails now, I
am lost. Sure enough, it was just as I had dreaded,
he started in to climb the tree —"

"What, the bull?"

"Of course — who else?"

"But a bull can't climb a tree."

"He can't, can't he? Since you know so much
about it, did you ever see a bull try?"

"No! I never dreamt of such a thing."

"Well, then, what is the use of your talking that
way, then? Because you never saw a thing done, is
that any reason why it can't be done?"

"Well, all right — go on. What did you do?"

"The bull started up, and got along well for
about ten feet, then slipped and slid back. I
breathed easier. He tried it again — got up a little
higher — slipped again. But he came at it once
more, and this time he was careful. He got gradually higher and higher, and my spirits went down
more and more. Up he came — an inch at a time
— with his eyes hot, and his tongue hanging out.
Higher and higher — hitched his foot over the stump
of a limb, and looked up, as much as to say, 'You
are my meat, friend.' Up again — higher and
higher, and getting more excited the closer he got.
He was within ten feet of me! I took a long breath,
— and then said I, 'It is now or never.' I had the
coil of the lariat all ready; I paid it out slowly, till it
hung right over his head; all of a sudden I let go of

the slack, and the slipnoose fell fairly round his neck! Quicker than lightning I out with the Allen and let him have it in the face. It was an awful roar, and must have scared the bull out of his senses. When the smoke cleared away, there he was, dangling in the air, twenty foot from the ground, and going out of one convulsion into another faster than you could count! I didn't stop to count, anyhow —I shinned down the tree and shot for home."

"Bemis, is all that true, just as you have stated it?"

"I wish I may rot in my tracks and die the death of a dog if it isn't."

"Well, we can't refuse to believe it, and we don't. But if there were some proofs —"

"Proofs! Did I bring back my lariat?"

"No."

"Did I bring back my horse?"

"No."

"Did you ever see the bull again?"

"No."

"Well, then, what more do you want? I never saw anybody as particular as you are about a little thing like that."

I made up my mind that if this man was not a liar he only missed it by the skin of his teeth. This episode reminds me of an incident of my brief sojourn in Siam, years afterward. The European citizens of a town in the neighborhood of Bangkok had a prodigy among them by the name of Eckert,

5*

an Englishman — a person famous for the number, ingenuity, and imposing magnitude of his lies. They were always repeating his most celebrated false-hoods, and always trying to " draw him out " before strangers; but they seldom succeeded. Twice he was invited to the house where I was visiting, but nothing could seduce him into a specimen lie. One day a planter named Bascom, an influential man, and a proud and sometimes irascible one, invited me to ride over with him and call on Eckert. As we jogged along, said he:

" Now, do you know where the fault lies? It lies in putting Eckert on his guard. The minute the boys go to pumping at Eckert he knows perfectly well what they are after, and of course he shuts up his shell. Anybody might know he would. But when we get there, we must play him finer than that. Let him shape the conversation to suit himself — let him drop it or change it whenever he wants to. Let him see that nobody is trying to draw him out. Just let him have his own way. He will soon forget himself and begin to grind out lies like a mill. Don't get impatient — just keep quiet, and let me play him. I will make him lie. It does seem to me that the boys must be blind to overlook such an obvious and simple trick as that."

Eckert received us heartily — a pleasant-spoken, gentle-mannered creature. We sat in the veranda an hour, sipping English ale, and talking about the king, and the sacred white elephant, the Sleeping

Idol, and all manner of things; and I noticed that
my comrade never led the conversation himself or
shaped it, but simply followed Eckert's lead, and
betrayed no solicitude and no anxiety about anything. The effect was shortly perceptible. Eckert
began to grow communicative; he grew more and
more at his ease, and more and more talkative and
sociable. Another hour passed in the same way, and
then all of a sudden Eckert said:

"Oh, by the way! I came near forgetting. I
have got a thing here to astonish you. Such a thing
as neither you nor any other man ever heard of —
I've got a cat that will eat cocoanut! Common
green cocoanut — and not only eat the meat, but
drink the milk. It is so — I'll swear to it."

A quick glance from Bascom — a glance that I
understood — then:

"Why, bless my soul, I never heard of such a
thing. Man, it is impossible."

"I knew you would say it. I'll fetch the cat."

He went in the house. Bascom said:

"There — what did I tell you? Now, that is the
way to handle Eckert. You see, I have petted him
along patiently, and put his suspicions to sleep. I
am glad we came. You tell the boys about it when
you go back. Cat eat a cocoanut — oh, my! Now,
that is just his way, exactly — he will tell the absurd-
est lie, and trust to luck to get out of it again. Cat
eat a cocoanut — the innocent fool!"

Eckert approached with his cat, sure enough.

E *

Bascom smiled.   Said he:

" I'll hold the cat — you bring a cocoanut."

Eckert split one open, and chopped up some pieces.   Bascom smuggled a wink to me, and proffered a slice of the fruit to puss.   She snatched it, swallowed it ravenously, and asked for more!

We rode our two miles in silence, and wide apart. At least I was silent, though Bascom cuffed his horse and cursed him a good deal, notwithstanding the horse was behaving well enough.   When I branched off homeward, Bascom said:

" Keep the horse till morning.   And — you need not speak of this —— foolishness to the boys."

CHAPTER VIII.

IN a little while all interest was taken up in stretching our necks and watching for the " pony-rider " — the fleet messenger who sped across the continent from St. Joe to Sacramento, carrying letters nineteen hundred miles in eight days! Think of that for perishable horse and human flesh and blood to do! The pony-rider was usually a little bit of a man, brimful of spirit and endurance. No matter what time of the day or night his watch came on, and no matter whether it was winter or summer, raining, snowing, hailing, or sleeting, or whether his " beat " was a level straight road or a crazy trail over mountain crags and precipices, or whether it led through peaceful regions or regions that swarmed with hostile Indians, he must be always ready to leap into the saddle and be off like the wind! There was no idling-time for a pony-rider on duty. He rode fifty miles without stopping, by daylight, moonlight, starlight, or through the blackness of darkness — just as it happened. He rode a splendid horse that was born for a racer and fed and lodged like a gentleman; kept him at his utmost speed for ten miles,

and then, as he came crashing up to the station
where stood two men holding fast a fresh, impatient
steed, the transfer of rider and mail-bag was made
in the twinkling of an eye, and away flew the eager
pair and were out of sight before the spectator could
get hardly the ghost of a look. Both rider and horse
went "flying light." The rider's dress was thin,
and fitted close; he wore a "roundabout," and a
skull-cap, and tucked his pantaloons into his boot-
tops like a race-rider. He carried no arms — he
carried nothing that was not absolutely necessary,
for even the postage on his literary freight was
worth *five dollars a letter*. He got but little frivol-
ous correspondence to carry — his bag had business
letters in it, mostly. His horse was stripped of all
unnecessary weight, too. He wore a little wafer of
a racing-saddle, and no visible blanket. He wore
light shoes, or none at all. The little flat mail-
pockets strapped under the rider's thighs would each
hold about the bulk of a child's primer. They held
many and many an important business chapter and
newspaper letter, but these were written on paper as
airy and thin as gold-leaf, nearly, and thus bulk and
weight were economized. The stage-coach traveled
about a hundred to a hundred and twenty-five miles
a day (twenty-four hours), the pony-rider about two
hundred and fifty. There were about eighty pony-
riders in the saddle all the time, night and day,
stretching in a long, scattering procession from Missouri to California, forty flying eastward, and forty

toward the west, and among them making four hundred gallant horses earn a stirring livelihood and see
a deal of scenery every single day in the year.

We had had a consuming desire, from the beginning, to see a pony-rider, but somehow or other all
that passed us and all that met us managed to streak
by in the night, and so we heard only a whiz and a
hail, and the swift phantom of the desert was gone
before we could get our heads out of the windows.
But now we were expecting one along every moment,
and would see him in broad daylight.   Presently the
driver exclaims:

" HERE HE COMES !"

Every neck is stretched further, and every eye
strained wider.   Away across the endless dead level
of the prairie a black speck appears against the sky,
and it is plain that it moves.   Well, I should think
so !   In a second or two it becomes a horse and
rider, rising and falling, rising and falling — sweeping toward us nearer and nearer — growing more and
more distinct, more and more sharply defined —
nearer and still nearer, and the flutter of the hoofs
comes faintly to the ear — another instant a whoop
and a hurrah from our upper deck, a wave of the
rider's hand, but no reply, and man and horse burst
past our excited faces, and go winging away like a
belated fragment of a storm !

So sudden is it all, and so like a flash of unreal
fancy, that but for the flake of white foam left quiv-
ering and perishing on a mail-sack after the vision

had flashed by and disappeared, we might have doubted whether we had seen any actual horse and man at all, maybe.

We rattled through Scott's Bluffs Pass, by and by. It was along here somewhere that we first came across genuine and unmistakable alkali water in the road, and we cordially hailed it as a first-class curiosity, and a thing to be mentioned with éclat in letters to the ignorant at home. This water gave the road a soapy appearance, and in many places the ground looked as if it had been whitewashed. I think the strange alkali water excited us as much as any wonder we had come upon yet, and I know we felt very complacent and conceited, and better satisfied with life after we had added it to our list of things which *we* had seen and some other people had not. In a small way we were the same sort of simpletons as those who climb unnecessarily the perilous peaks of Mont Blanc and the Matterhorn, and derive no pleasure from it except the reflection that it isn't a common experience. But once in a while one of those parties trips and comes darting down the long mountain-crags in a sitting-posture, making the crusted snow smoke behind him, flitting from bench to bench, and from terrace to terrace, jarring the earth where he strikes, and still glancing and flitting on again, sticking an iceberg into himself every now and then, and tearing his clothes, snatching at things to save himself, taking hold of trees and fetching them along with him, roots and all, starting little rocks now and then, then big boulders, then acres of ice and snow and patches of forest, gathering and still gathering as he goes, and adding and still adding to his massed and sweeping grandeur as he nears a three-thousand-foot precipice, till at last he waves his hat magnificently and rides into eternity on the back of a raging and tossing avalanche!

This is all very fine, but let us not be carried away by excitement, but ask calmly, how does this person feel about it in his cooler moments next day, with six or seven thousand feet of snow and stuff on top of him?

We crossed the sand hills near the scene of the Indian mail robbery and massacre of 1856, wherein the driver and conductor perished, and also all the passengers but one, it was supposed; but this must have been a mistake, for at different times afterward on the Pacific coast I was personally acquainted with a hundred and thirty-three or four people who were wounded during that massacre, and barely escaped with their lives. There was no doubt of the truth of it — I had it from their own lips. One of these parties told me that he kept coming across arrowheads in his system for nearly seven years after the massacre; and another of them told me that he was stuck so literally full of arrows that after the Indians were gone and he could raise up and examine himself, he could not restrain his tears, for his clothes were completely ruined.

The most trustworthy tradition avers, however,
that only one man, a person named Babbitt, survived
the massacre, and he was desperately wounded. He
dragged himself on his hands and knee (for one leg
was broken) to a station several miles away. He
did it during portions of two nights, lying concealed
one day and part of another, and for more than
forty hours suffering unimaginable anguish from
hunger, thirst, and bodily pain. The Indians robbed
the coach of everything it contained, including quite
an amount of treasure.

CHAPTER IX.

WE passed Fort Laramie in the night, and on the seventh morning out we found ourselves in the Black Hills, with Laramie Peak at our elbow (apparently) looming vast and solitary — a deep, dark, rich indigo blue in hue, so portentously did the old colossus frown under his beetling brows of storm-cloud. He was thirty or forty miles away, in reality, but he only seemed removed a little beyond the low ridge at our right. We breakfasted at Horse-Shoe Station, six hundred and seventy-six miles out from St. Joseph. We had now reached a hostile Indian country, and during the afternoon we passed Laparelle Station, and enjoyed great discomfort all the time we were in the neighborhood, being aware that many of the trees we dashed by at arm's length concealed a lurking Indian or two. During the preceding night an ambushed savage had sent a bullet through the pony-rider's jacket, but he had ridden on, just the same, because pony-riders were not allowed to stop and inquire into such things except when killed. As long as they had life enough left in them they had to stick to the horse and ride, even

6

if the Indians had been waiting for them a week, and were entirely out of patience. About two hours and a half before we arrived at Laparelle Station, the keeper in charge of it had fired four times at an Indian, but he said with an injured air that the Indian had " skipped around so's to spile everything — and ammunition's blamed skurse, too." The most natural inference conveyed by his manner of speaking was, that in " skipping around," the Indian had taken an unfair advantage. The coach we were in had a neat hole through its front — a reminiscence of its last trip through this region. The bullet that made it wounded the driver slightly, but he did not mind it much. He said the place to keep a man " huffy " was down on the Southern Overland, among the Apaches, before the company moved the stage line up on the northern route. He said the Apaches used to annoy him all the time down there, and that he came as near as anything to starving to death in the midst of abundance, because they kept him so leaky with bullet holes that he " couldn't hold his vittles." This person's statements were not generally believed.

We shut the blinds down very tightly that first night in the hostile Indian country, and lay on our arms. We slept on them some, but most of the time we only lay on them. We did not talk much, but kept quiet and listened. It was an inky-black night, and occasionally rainy. We were among woods and rocks, hills and gorges — so shut in, in fact, that when we peeped through a chink in a curtain, we could discern nothing. The driver and conductor on top were still, too, or only spoke at long intervals, in low tones, as is the way of men in the midst of invisible dangers. We listened to rain-drops pattering on the roof; and the grinding of the wheels through the muddy gravel; and the low wailing of the wind; and all the time we had that absurd sense upon us, inseparable from travel at night in a close-curtained vehicle, the sense of remaining perfectly still in one place, notwithstanding the jolting and swaying of the vehicle, the trampling of the horses, and the grinding of the wheels. We listened a long time, with intent faculties and bated breath; every time one of us would relax, and draw a long sigh of relief and start to say something, a comrade would be sure to utter a sudden " Hark!" and instantly the experimenter was rigid and listening again. So the tiresome minutes and decades of minutes dragged away, until at last our tense forms filmed over with a dulled consciousness, and we slept, if one might call such a condition by so strong a name — for it was a sleep set with a hair-trigger. It was a sleep seething and teeming with a weird and distressful confusion of shreds and fag-ends of dreams — a sleep that was a chaos. Presently, dreams and sleep and the sullen hush of the night were startled by a ringing report, and cloven by *such* a long, wild, agonizing shriek! Then we heard — ten steps from the stage —

"Help! help! help!" [It was our driver's voice.]

"Kill him! Kill him like a dog!"

"I'm being murdered! Will no man lend me a pistol?"

"Look out! head him off! head him off!"

[Two pistol shots; a confusion of voices and the trampling of many feet, as if a crowd were closing and surging together around some object; several heavy, dull blows, as with a club; a voice that said appealingly, "Don't, gentlemen, please don't — I'm a dead man!" Then a fainter groan, and another blow, and away sped the stage into the darkness, and left the grisly mystery behind us.]

What a startle it was! Eight seconds would amply cover the time it occupied — maybe even five would do it. We only had time to plunge at a curtain and unbuckle and unbutton part of it in an awkward and hindering flurry, when our whip cracked sharply overhead, and we went rumbling and thundering away, down a mountain "grade."

We fed on that mystery the rest of the night — what was left of it, for it was waning fast. It had to remain a present mystery, for all we could get from the conductor in answer to our hails was something that sounded, through the clatter of the wheels, like "Tell you in the morning!"

So we lit our pipes and opened the corner of a curtain for a chimney, and lay there in the dark, listening to each other's story of how he first felt and how many thousand Indians he first thought had hurled themselves upon us, and what his remembrance of the subsequent sounds was, and the order of their occurrence. And we theorized, too, but there was never a theory that would account for our driver's voice being out there, nor yet account for his Indian murderers talking such good English, if they *were* Indians.

So we chatted and smoked the rest of the night comfortably away, our boding anxiety being somehow marvelously dissipated by the real presence of something to be anxious *about*.

We never did get much satisfaction about that dark occurrence. All that we could make out of the odds and ends of the information we gathered in the morning, was that the disturbance occurred at a station; that we changed drivers there, and that the driver that got off there had been talking roughly about some of the outlaws that infested the region ("for there wasn't a man around there but had a price on his head and didn't dare show himself in the settlements," the conductor said); he had talked roughly about these characters, and ought to have "drove up there with his pistol cocked and ready on the seat alongside of him, and begun business himself, because any softy would know they would be laying for him."

That was all we could gather, and we could see that neither the conductor nor the new driver were much concerned about the matter. They plainly

had little respect for a man who would deliver offensive opinions of people and then be so simple as to
come into their presence unprepared to " back his
judgment," as they pleasantly phrased the killing of
any fellow-being who did not like said opinions.   And
likewise they plainly had a contempt for the man's
poor discretion in venturing to rouse the wrath of
such utterly reckless wild beasts as those outlaws —
and the conductor added:

"I tell you it's as much as Slade himself wants
to do!"

This remark created an entire revolution in my curiosity.   I cared nothing now about the Indians, and
even lost interest in the murdered driver.   There was
much magic in that name, SLADE!   Day or night,
now, I stood always ready to drop any subject in hand,
to listen to something new about Slade and his ghastly
exploits.   Even before we got to Overland City, we
had begun to hear about Slade and his " division "
(for he was a " division-agent ") on the Overland;
and from the hour we had left Overland City we had
heard drivers and conductors talk about only three
things — " Californy," the Nevada silver mines, and
this desperado Slade.   And a deal the most of
the talk was about Slade.   We had gradually come
to have a realizing sense of the fact that Slade was a
man whose heart and hands and soul were steeped
in the blood of offenders against his dignity; a man
who awfully avenged all injuries, affronts, insults or
slights, of whatever kind — on the spot if he could,

years afterward if lack of earlier opportunity compelled it; a man whose hate tortured him day and night till vengeance appeased it — and not an ordinary vengeance either, but his enemy's absolute death — nothing less; a man whose face would light up with a terrible joy when he surprised a foe and had him at a disadvantage.   A high and efficient servant of the Overland, an outlaw among outlaws and yet their relentless scourge, Slade was at once the most bloody, the most dangerous, and the most valuable citizen that inhabited the savage fastnesses of the mountains.

CHAPTER X.

REALLY and truly, two-thirds of the talk of drivers and conductors had been about this man
Slade, ever since the day before we reached Julesburg. In order that the Eastern reader may have
a clear conception of what a Rocky Mountain
desperado is, in his highest state of development,
I will reduce all this mass of overland gossip to one
straightforward narrative, and present it in the following shape:

Slade was born in Illinois, of good parentage. At
about twenty-six years of age he killed a man in a
quarrel and fled the country. At St. Joseph, Missouri, he joined one of the early California-bound
emigrant trains, and was given the post of train-
master. One day on the plains he had an angry
dispute with one of his wagon-drivers, and both drew
their revolvers. But the driver was the quicker
artist, and had his weapon cocked first. So Slade
said it was a pity to waste life on so small a matter,
and proposed that the pistols be thrown on the
ground and the quarrel settled by a fist-fight. The
unsuspecting driver agreed, and threw down his

pistol — whereupon Slade laughed at his simplicity, and shot him dead!

He made his escape, and lived a wild life for awhile, dividing his time between fighting Indians and avoiding an Illinois sheriff, who had been sent to arrest him for his first murder. It is said that in one Indian battle he killed three savages with his own hand, and afterward cut their ears off and sent them, with his compliments, to the chief of the tribe.

Slade soon gained a name for fearless resolution, and this was sufficient merit to procure for him the important post of overland division-agent at Jules-burg, in place of Mr. Jules, removed. For some time previously, the company's horses had been fre-quently stolen, and the coaches delayed, by gangs of outlaws, who were wont to laugh at the idea of any man's having the temerity to resent such out-rages. Slade resented them promptly. The out-laws soon found that the new agent was a man who did not fear anything that breathed the breath of life. He made short work of all offenders. The result was that delays ceased, the company's property was let alone, and, no matter what happened or who suffered, Slade's coaches went through, every time! True, in order to bring about this wholesome change, Slade had to kill several men — some say three, others say four, and others six — but the world was the richer for their loss. The first prominent difficulty he had was with the ex-agent Jules, who bore the reputation of being a reck-

F.

less and desperate man himself. Jules hated Slade
for supplanting him, and a good fair occasion for a
fight was all he was waiting for. By and by Slade
dared to employ a man whom Jules had once discharged. Next, Slade seized a team of stage-horses
which he accused Jules of having driven off and hidden somewhere for his own use. War was declared,
and for a day or two the two men walked warily
about the streets, seeking each other, Jules armed
with a double-barreled shot gun, and Slade with his
history-creating revolver. Finally, as Slade stepped
into a store, Jules poured the contents of his gun
into him from behind the door. Slade was pluck,
and Jules got several bad pistol wounds in return.
Then both men fell, and were carried to their respect-
ive lodgings, both swearing that better aim should do
deadlier work next time. Both were bed-ridden a
long time, but Jules got on his feet first, and gathering his possessions together, packed them on a
couple of mules, and fled to the Rocky Mountains to
gather strength in safety against the day of reckon-
ing. For many months he was not seen or heard
of, and was gradually dropped out of the remembrance of all save Slade himself. But Slade was
not the man to forget him. On the contrary, common report said that Slade kept a reward standing
for his capture, dead or alive!

After awhile, seeing that Slade's energetic administration had restored peace and order to one of the
worst divisions of the road, the Overland Stage Com-

pany transferred him to the Rocky Ridge division
in the Rocky Mountains, to see if he could perform
a like miracle there. It was the very paradise of outlaws and desperadoes. There was absolutely no
semblance of law there. Violence was the rule.
Force was the only recognized authority. The com-
monest misunderstandings were settled on the spot
with the revolver or the knife. Murders were done
in open day, and with sparkling frequency, and nobody thought of inquiring into them. It was considered that the parties who did the killing had their
private reasons for it; for other people to meddle
would have been looked upon as indelicate. After
a murder, all that Rocky Mountain etiquette required
of a spectator was, that he should help the gentlemen bury his game — otherwise his churlishness
would surely be remembered against him the first
time he killed a man himself and needed a neighborly
turn in interring him.

Slade took up his residence sweetly and peacefully
in the midst of this hive of horse-thieves and assassins, and the very first time one of them aired his insolent swaggerings in his presence he shot him dead!
He began a raid on the outlaws, and in a singularly
short space of time he had completely stopped their
depredations on the stage stock, recovered a large
number of stolen horses, killed several of the worst
desperadoes of the district, and gained such a dread
ascendancy over the rest that they respected him,
admired him, feared him, obeyed him! He wrought

the same marvelous change in the ways of the community that had marked his administration at Overland City.   He captured two men who had stolen Overland stock, and with his own hands he hanged them.   He was supreme judge in his district, and he was jury and executioner likewise — and not only in the case of offenses against his employers, but against passing emigrants as well.   On one occasion some emigrants had their stock lost or stolen, and told Slade, who chanced to visit their camp.   With a single companion he rode to a ranch, the owners of which he suspected, and, opening the door, commenced firing, killing three, and wounding the fourth.

From a bloodthirstily interesting little Montana book* I take this paragraph:

While on the road, Slade held absolute sway.   He would ride down to a station, get into a quarrel, turn the house out of windows, and maltreat the occupants most cruelly.   The unfortunates had no means of redress, and were compelled to recuperate as best they could.   On one of these occasions, it is said he killed the father of the fine little half-breed boy Jemmy, whom he adopted, and who lived with his widow after his execution.   Stories of Slade's hanging men, and of innumerable assaults, shootings, stabbings, and beatings, in which he was a principal actor, form part of the legends of the stage line.   As for minor quarrels and shootings, it is absolutely certain that a minute history of Slade's life would be one long record of such practices.

Slade was a matchless marksman with a navy revolver.   The legends say that one morning at Rocky Ridge, when he was feeling comfortable, he saw a

_____

* "The Vigilantes of Montana," by Prof. Thos. J. Dimsdale.

man approaching who had offended him some days
before — observe the fine memory he had for matters like that — and, "Gentlemen," said Slade, drawing, "it is a good twenty-yard shot—I'll clip the
third button on his coat!" Which he did. The
bystanders all admired it. And they all attended
the funeral, too.

On one occasion a man who kept a little whisky-
shelf at the station did something which angered
Slade — and went and made his will. A day or two
afterward Slade came in and called for some brandy.
The man reached under the counter (ostensibly to
get a bottle — possibly to get something else), but
Slade smiled upon him that peculiarly bland and satisfied smile of his which the neighbors had long ago
learned to recognize as a death warrant in disguise,
and told him to "none of that! — pass out the high-
priced article." So the poor barkeeper had to turn
his back and get the high-priced brandy from the
shelf; and when he faced around again he was looking into the muzzle of Slade's pistol. "And the
next instant," added my informant, impressively,
"he was one of the deadest men that ever lived."

The stage drivers and conductors told us that sometimes Slade would leave a hated enemy wholly un-
molested, unnoticed and unmentioned, for weeks together — had done it once or twice, at any rate.
And some said they believed he did it in order to
lull the victims into unwatchfulness, so that he could
get the advantage of them, and others said they

believed he saved up an enemy that way, just as a
schoolboy saves up a cake, and made the pleasure
go as far as it would by gloating over the anticipation.   One of these cases was that of a Frenchman
who had offended Slade.   To the surprise of everybody Slade did not kill him on the spot, but let him
alone for a considerable time.   Finally, however, he
went to the Frenchman's house very late one night,
knocked, and when his enemy opened the door, shot
him dead — pushed the corpse inside the door with
his foot, set the house on fire and burned up the
dead man, his widow and three children!   I heard
this story from several different people, and they
evidently believed what they were saying.   It may
be true, and it may not.   " Give a dog a bad
name," etc.

Slade was captured once, by a party of men who
intended to lynch him.   They disarmed him, and
shut him up in a strong log-house, and placed a
guard over him.   He prevailed on his captors to
send for his wife, so that he might have a last inter-
view with her.   She was a brave, loving, spirited
woman.   She jumped on a horse and rode for life
and death.   When she arrived they let her in without searching her, and before the door could be
closed she whipped out a couple of revolvers, and
she and her lord marched forth defying the party.
And then, under a brisk fire, they mounted double
and galloped away unharmed!

In the fullness of time Slade's myrmidons captured

his ancient enemy, Jules, whom they found in a well-chosen hiding-place in the remote fastnesses of the mountains, gaining a precarious livelihood with his rifle. They brought him to Rocky Ridge, bound hand and foot, and deposited him in the middle of the cattle-yard with his back against a post. It is said that the pleasure that lit Slade's face when he heard of it was something fearful to contemplate. He examined his enemy to see that he was securely tied, and then went to bed, content to wait till morning before enjoying the luxury of killing him. Jules spent the night in the cattle-yard, and it is a region where warm nights are never known. In the morning Slade practised on him with his revolver, nipping the flesh here and there, and occasionally clipping off a finger, while Jules begged him to kill him outright and put him out of his misery. Finally Slade reloaded, and walking up close to his victim, made some characteristic remarks and then dispatched him. The body lay there half a day, nobody venturing to touch it without orders, and then Slade detailed a party and assisted at the burial himself. But he first cut off the dead man's ears and put them in his vest pocket, where he carried them for some time with great satisfaction. That is the story as I have frequently heard it told and seen it in print in California newspapers. It is doubtless correct in all essential particulars.

In due time we rattled up to a stage-station, and sat down to breakfast with a half-savage, half-civilized company of armed and bearded mountaineers, ranchmen and station employés. The most gentle-manly-appearing, quiet, and affable officer we had yet found along the road in the Overland Company's service was the person who sat at the head of the table, at my elbow. Never youth stared and shivered as I did when I heard them call him SLADE!

Here was romance, and I sitting face to face with it!—looking upon it—touching it—hobnob-bing with it, as it were! Here, right by my side, was the actual ogre who, in fights and brawls and various ways, *had taken the lives of twenty-six human beings*, or all men lied about him! I suppose I was the proudest stripling that ever traveled to see strange lands and wonderful people.

He was so friendly and so gentle-spoken that I warmed to him in spite of his awful history. It was hardly possible to realize that this pleasant person was the pitiless scourge of the outlaws, the raw-head-and-bloody-bones the nursing mothers of the mountains terrified their children with. And to this day I can remember nothing remarkable about Slade except that his face was rather broad across the cheek bones, and that the cheek bones were low and the lips peculiarly thin and straight. But that was enough to leave something of an effect upon me, for since then I seldom see a face possessing those characteristics without fancying that the owner of it is a dangerous man.

The coffee ran out. At least it was reduced to

HERE WAS ROMANCE

one tin-cupful, and Slade was about to take it when he saw that my cup was empty. He politely offered to fill it, but although I wanted it, I politely declined. I was afraid he had not killed anybody that morning, and might be needing diversion. But still with firm politeness he insisted on filling my cup, and said I had traveled all night and better deserved it than he — and while he talked he placidly poured the fluid, to the last drop. I thanked him and drank it, but it gave me no comfort, for I could not feel sure that he would not be sorry, presently, that he had given it away, and proceed to kill me to distract his thoughts from the loss. But nothing of the kind occurred. We left him with only twenty-six dead people to account for, and I felt a tranquil satisfaction in the thought that in so judiciously taking care of No. 1 at that breakfast-table I had pleasantly escaped being No. 27. Slade came out to the coach and saw us off, first ordering certain rearrangements of the mail-bags for our comfort, and then we took leave of him, satisfied that we should hear of him again, some day, and wondering in what connection.

7

CHAPTER XI.

AND sure enough, two or three years afterward, we did hear of him again. News came to the Pacific coast that the Vigilance Committee in Montana (whither Slade had removed from Rocky Ridge) had hanged him. I find an account of the affair in the thrilling little book I quoted a paragraph from in the last chapter — " The Vigilantes of Montana; being a Reliable Account of the Capture, Trial and Execution of Henry Plummer's Notorious Road Agent Band: By Prof. Thos. J. Dimsdale, Virginia City, M. T." Mr. Dimsdale's chapter is well worth reading, as a specimen of how the people of the frontier deal with criminals when the courts of law prove inefficient. Mr. Dimsdale makes two remarks about Slade, both of which are accurately descriptive, and one of which is exceedingly picturesque: " Those who saw him in his natural state only, would pronounce him to be a kind husband, a most hospitable host, and a courteous gentleman; on the contrary, those who met him when maddened with liquor and surrounded by a gang of armed roughs, would pronounce him a fiend incarnate." And this: " From Fort Kearney, west, he was feared

(92)

a great deal more than the Almighty.'' For com-
pactness, simplicity, and vigor of expression, I will
'' back '' that sentence against anything in litera-
ture.   Mr. Dimsdale's narrative is as follows.   In
all places where italics occur they are mine:

After the execution of the five men on the 14th of January, the
Vigilantes considered that their work was nearly ended.   They had
freed the country of highwaymen and murderers to a great extent, and
they determined that in the absence of the regular civil authority they
would establish a People's Court where all offenders should be tried by
judge and jury.   This was the nearest approach to social order that the
circumstances permitted, and, though strict legal authority was wanting,
yet the people were firmly determined to maintain its efficiency, and to
enforce its decrees.   It may here be mentioned that the overt act which
was the last round on the fatal ladder leading to the scaffold on which
Slade perished, *was the tearing in pieces and stamping upon a writ of
this court, followed by his arrest of the Judge, Alex. Davis, by authority
of a presented Derringer, and with his own hands.*

J. A. Slade was himself, we have been informed, a Vigilante ; he
openly boasted of it, and said he knew all that they knew.   He was never
accused, or even suspected, of either murder or robbery, committed in
this Territory (the latter crime was never laid to his charge, in any
place); but that he had killed several men in other localities was notorious, and his bad reputation in this respect was a most powerful argument in determining his fate, when he was finally arrested for the of-
fense above mentioned.   On returning from Milk River he became
more and more addicted to drinking, until at last it was a common feat
for him and his friends to ''take the town.''   He and a couple of his
dependents might often be seen on one horse, galloping through the
streets, shouting and yelling, firing revolvers, etc.   On many occasions
he would ride his horse into stores, break up bars, toss the scales out of
doors, and use most insulting language to parties present.   Just previous
to the day of his arrest, he had given a fearful beating to one of his
followers; but such was his influence over them that the man wept bitterly at the gallows, and begged for his life with all his power.   *It had
become quite common, when Slade was on a spree, for the shopkeepers
and citizens to close the stores and put out all the lights;* being fearful
of some outrage at his hands.   For his wanton destruction of goods and

furniture, he was always ready to pay, when sober, if he had money; but there were not a few who regarded payment as small satisfaction for the outrage, and these men were his personal enemies.

From time to time Slade received warnings from men that he well knew would not deceive him, of the certain end of his conduct. There was not a moment, for weeks previous to his arrest, in which the public did not expect to hear of some bloody outrage. The dread of his very name, and the presence of the armed band of hangers-on who followed him alone prevented a resistance which must certainly have ended in the instant murder or mutilation of the opposing party.

Slade was frequently arrested by order of the court whose organization we have described, and had treated it with respect by paying one or two fines and promising to pay the rest when he had money; but in the transaction that occurred at this crisis, he forgot even this caution, and, goaded by passion and the hatred of restraint, he sprang into the embrace of death.

Slade had been drunk and "cutting-up" all night. He and his companions had made the town a perfect hell. In the morning, J. M. Fox, the sheriff, met him, arrested him, took him into court and commenced reading a warrant that he had for his arrest, by way of arraignment. He became uncontrollably furious, and *seizing the writ, he tore it up, threw it on the ground and stamped upon it.* The clicking of the locks of his companions' revolvers was instantly heard, and a crisis was expected. The sheriff did not attempt his retention; but being at least as prudent as he was valiant, he succumbed, leaving Slade the *master of the situation and the conqueror and ruler of the courts, law, and law-makers.* This was a declaration of war, and was so accepted. The Vigilance Committee now felt that the question of social order and the preponderance of the law-abiding citizens had then and there to be decided. They knew the character of Slade, and they were well aware that they must submit to his rule without murmur, or else that he must be dealt with in such fashion as would prevent his being able to wreak his vengeance on the committee, who could never have hoped to live in the Territory secure from outrage or death, and who could never leave it without encountering his friends, whom his victory would have emboldened and stimulated to a pitch that would have rendered them reckless of consequences. The day previous he had ridden into Dorris's store, and, on being requested to leave, he drew his revolver and threatened to kill the gentleman who spoke to him. Another saloon he had led his horse into, and, buying a bottle of wine, he tried to make the animal drink it. This was not considered an uncommon performance, as he had often entered saloons and commenced firing at the lamps, causing a wild stampede.

A leading member of the committee met Slade, and informed him in the quiet, earnest manner of one who feels the importance of what he is saying: "Slade, get your horse at once, and go home, or there will be ――― to pay." Slade started and took a long look, with his dark and piercing eyes, at the gentleman. "What do you mean?" said he. "You have no right to ask what I mean," was the quiet reply, "get your horse at once, and remember what I tell you." After a short pause he promised to do so, and actually got into the saddle; but, being still intoxicated, he began calling aloud to one after another of his friends, and at last seemed to have forgotten the warning he had received and became again uproarious, shouting the name of a wellknown courtezan in company with those of two men whom he considered heads of the committee, as a sort of challenge; perhaps, however, as a simple act of bravado. It seems probable that the intimation of personal danger he had received had not been forgotten entirely; though, fatally for him, he took a foolish way of showing his remembrance of it. He sought out Alexander Davis, the Judge of the Court, and, drawing a cocked Derringer, he presented it at his head, and told him that he should hold him as a hostage for his own safety. As the judge stood perfectly quiet, and offered no resistance to his captor, no further outrage followed on this score. Previous to this, on account of the critical state of affairs, the committee had met, and at last resolved to arrest him. His execution had not been agreed upon, and, at that time, would have been negatived, most assuredly. A messenger rode down to Nevada to inform the leading men of what was on hand, as it was desirable to show that there was a feeling of unanimity on the subject, all along the gulch.

The miners turned out almost *en masse*, leaving their work and forming in solid column, about six hundred strong, armed to the teeth, they marched up to Virginia. The leader of the body well knew the temper of his men on the subject. He spurred on ahead of them, and, hastily calling a meeting of the executive, he told them plainly that the miners meant "business," and that, if they came up, they would not stand in the street to be shot down by Slade's friends; but that they would take him and hang him. The meeting was small, as the Virginia men were loath to act at all. This momentous announcement of the feeling of the Lower Town was made to a cluster of men, who were deliberating behind a wagon, at the rear of a store on Main street.

The committee were most unwilling to proceed to extremities. All the duty they had ever performed seemed as nothing to the task before them; but they had to decide, and that quickly. It was finally agreed that if the whole body of the miners were of the opinion that he should be hanged, that the committee left it in their hands to deal with him. Off, at hot speed, rode the leader of the Nevada men to join his command.

Slade had found out what was intended, and the news sobered him instantly. He went into P. S. Pfouts' store, where Davis was, and apologized for his conduct, saying that he would take it all back.

The head of the column now wheeled into Wallace street and marched up at quick time. Halting in front of the store, the executive officer of the committee stepped forward and arrested Slade, who was at once informed of his doom, and inquiry was made as to whether he had any business to settle. Several parties spoke to him on the subject; but to all such inquiries he turned a deaf ear, being entirely absorbed in the terrifying reflections on his own awful position. He never ceased his entreaties for life, and to see his dear wife. The unfortunate lady referred to, between whom and Slade there existed a warm affection, was at this time living at their ranch on the Madison. She was possessed of considerable personal attractions; tall, well-formed, of graceful carriage, pleasing manners, and was, withal, an accomplished horsewoman.

A messenger from Slade rode at full speed to inform her of her husband's arrest. In an instant she was in the saddle, and with all the energy that love and despair could lend to an ardent temperament and a strong physique, she urged her fleet charger over the twelve miles of rough and rocky ground that intervened between her and the object of her passionate devotion.

Meanwhile, a party of volunteers had made the necessary preparations for the execution, in the valley traversed by the branch. Beneath the site of Pfouts and Russell's stone building there was a corral, the gate-posts of which were strong and high. Across the top was laid a beam, to which the rope was fastened, and a dry-goods box served for the platform. To this place Slade was marched, surrounded by a guard, composing the best armed and most numerous force that has ever appeared in Montana Territory.

The doomed man had so exhausted himself by tears, prayers, and lamentations, that he had scarcely strength left to stand under the fatal beam. He repeatedly exclaimed, "My God! my God! must I die? Oh, my dear wife!"

On the return of the fatigue party, they encountered some friends of Slade, staunch and reliable citizens and members of the committee, but who were personally attached to the condemned. On hearing of his sentence, one of them, a stout-hearted man, pulled out his handkerchief and walked away, weeping like a child. Slade still begged to see his wife, most piteously, and it seemed hard to deny his request ; but the bloody consequences that were sure to follow the inevitable attempt at a rescue, that her presence and entreaties would have certainly incited, forbade the granting of his request. Several gentlemen were sent for to see him, in his last moments, one of whom (Judge Davis) made a short address to the people; but in such low tones as to be inaudible, save to a few in his immediate vicinity. One of his friends, after exhausting his powers of entreaty, threw off his coat and declared that the prisoner could not be hanged until he himself was killed. A hundred guns were instantly leveled at him; whereupon he turned and fled ; but, being brought back, he was compelled to resume his coat, and to give a promise of future peaceable demeanor.

Scarcely a leading man in Virginia could be found, though numbers of the citizens joined the ranks of the guard when the arrest was made. All lamented the stern necessity which dictated the execution.

Everything being ready, the command was given, "Men, do your duty," and the box being instantly slipped from beneath his feet, he died almost instantaneously.

The body was cut down and carried to the Virginia Hotel, where, in a darkened room, it was scarcely laid out, when the unfortunate and bereaved companion of the deceased arrived, at headlong speed, to find that all was over, and that she was a widow. Her grief and heart-piercing cries were terrible evidences of the depth of her attachment for her lost husband, and a considerable period elapsed before she could regain the command of her excited feelings.

There is something about the desperado-nature that is wholly unaccountable—at least it looks unaccountable. It is this. The true desperado is gifted with splendid courage, and yet he will take the most

7*

infamous advantage of his enemy; armed and free, he will stand up before a host and fight until he is shot all to pieces, and yet when he is under the gallows and helpless he will cry and plead like a child. Words are cheap, and it **is** easy to call Slade a coward (all executed men who do not " die game " are promptly called cowards by unreflecting people), and when we read of Slade that he " had so exhausted himself by tears, prayers, and lamentations, that he had scarcely strength left to stand under the fatal beam," the disgraceful word suggests itself in a moment — yet in frequently defying and inviting the vengeance of banded Rocky Mountain cut-throats by shooting down their comrades and leaders, and never offering to hide or fly, Slade showed that he was a man of peerless bravery. No coward would dare that. Many a notorious coward, many a chicken-livered poltroon, coarse, brutal, degraded, has made his dying speech without a quaver in his voice and been swung into eternity with what looked like the calmest fortitude, and so we are justified in believing, from the low intellect of such a creature, that it was not *moral* courage that enabled him to do it. Then, if moral courage is not the requisite quality, what could it have been that this stout-hearted Slade lacked? — this bloody, desperate, kindly-mannered, urbane gentleman, who never hesitated to warn his most ruffianly enemies that he would kill them whenever or wherever he came across them next! I think it is a conundrum worth investigating.

CHAPTER XII.

JUST beyond the breakfast-station we overtook a Mormon emigrant train of thirty-three wagons; and tramping wearily along and driving their herd of loose cows, were dozens of coarse-clad and sad-looking men, women, and children, who had walked as they were walking now, day after day for eight lingering weeks, and in that time had compassed the distance our stage had come in *eight days and three hours* — seven hundred and ninety-eight miles! They were dusty and uncombed, hatless, bonnetless, and ragged, and they did look so tired!

After breakfast, we bathed in Horse Creek, a (previously) limpid, sparkling stream — an appreciated luxury, for it was very seldom that our furious coach halted long enough for an indulgence of that kind. We changed horses ten or twelve times in every twenty-four hours — changed mules, rather — six mules — and did it nearly every time in *four minutes*. It was lively work. As our coach rattled up to each station six harnessed mules stepped gaily from the stable; and in the twinkling of an eye, almost, the old team was out and the new one in and we off and away again.

During the afternoon we passed Sweetwater Creek, Independence Rock, Devil's Gate, and the Devil's Gap. The latter were wild specimens of rugged scenery, and full of interest — *we were in the heart of the Rocky Mountains, now*. And we also passed by "Alkali" or "Soda Lake," and we woke up to the fact that our journey had stretched a long way across the world when the driver said that the Mormons often came there from Great Salt Lake City to haul away saleratus. He said that a few days gone by they had shoveled up enough pure saleratus from the ground (it was a *dry* lake) to load two wagons, and that when they got these two wagon-loads of a drug that cost them nothing, to Salt Lake, they could sell it for twenty-five cents a pound.

In the night we sailed by a most notable curiosity, and one we had been hearing a good deal about for a day or two, and were suffering to see. This was what might be called a natural ice-house. It was August, now, and sweltering weather in the daytime, yet at one of the stations the men could scrape the soil on the hillside under the lee of a range of boulders, and at a depth of six inches cut out pure blocks of ice — hard, compactly frozen, and clear as crystal!

Toward dawn we got under way again, and presently, as we sat with raised curtains enjoying our early-morning smoke and contemplating the first splendor of the rising sun as it swept down the long array of mountain peaks, flushing and gilding crag after crag

and summit after summit, as if the invisible Creator
reviewed his gray veterans and they saluted with a
smile, we hove in sight of South Pass City. The
hotel-keeper, the postmaster, the blacksmith, the
mayor, the constable, the city marshal, and the principal citizen and property-holder, all came out and
greeted us cheerily, and we gave him good day. He
gave us a little Indian news, and a little Rocky Mountain news, and we gave him some Plains information
in return. He then retired to his lonely grandeur
and we climbed on up among the bristling peaks and
the ragged clouds. South Pass City consisted of
four log cabins, one of which was unfinished, and the
gentleman with all those offices and titles was the
chiefest of the ten citizens of the place. Think of
hotel-keeper, postmaster, blacksmith, mayor, constable, city marshal and principal citizen all condensed
into one person and crammed into one skin. Bemis
said he was " a perfect Allen's revolver of dignities."
And he said that if he were to die as postmaster,
or as blacksmith, or as postmaster and blacksmith
both, the people might stand it; but if he were to
die all over, it would be a frightful loss to the community.

Two miles beyond South Pass City we saw for
the first time that mysterious marvel which all Western untraveled boys have heard of and fully believe
in, but are sure to be astounded at when they see it
with their own eyes, nevertheless — banks of snow in
dead summer time. We were now far up toward the

sky, and knew all the time that we must presently encounter lofty summits clad in the " eternal snow " which was so commonplace a matter of mention in books, and yet when I did see it glittering in the sun on stately domes in the distance and knew the month was August and that my coat was hanging up because it was too warm to wear it, I was full as much amazed as if I never had heard of snow in August before.   Truly, " seeing is believing " — and many a man lives a long life through, *thinking* he believes certain universally received and well established things, and yet never suspects that if he were confronted by those things once, he would discover that he did not *really* believe them before, but only thought he believed them.

In a little while quite a number of peaks swung into view with long claws of glittering snow clasping them; and with here and there, in the shade, down the mountain side, a little solitary patch of snow looking no larger than a lady's pocket-handkerchief but being in reality as large as a " public square."

And now, at last, we were fairly in the renowned SOUTH PASS, and whirling gaily along high above the common world.   We were perched upon the extreme summit of the great range of the Rocky Mountains, toward which we had been climbing, patiently climbing, ceaselessly climbing, for days and nights together — and about us was gathered a convention of Nature's kings that stood ten, twelve, and even thirteen thousand feet high — grand old fellows who

would have to stoop to see Mount Washington, in
the twilight. We were in such an airy elevation
above the creeping populations of the earth, that
now and then when the obstructing crags stood out
of the way it seemed that we could look around and
abroad and contemplate the whole great globe, with
its dissolving views of mountains, seas, and continents
stretching away through the mystery of the summer
haze.

As a general thing the Pass was more suggestive
of a valley than a suspension bridge in the clouds —
but it strongly suggested the latter at one spot. At
that place the upper third of one or two majestic purple domes projected above our level on either hand
and gave us a sense of a hidden great deep of mountains and plains and valleys down about their bases
which we fancied we might see if we could step to
the edge and look over. These Sultans of the fastnesses were turbaned with tumbled volumes of cloud,
which shredded away from time to time and drifted
off fringed and torn, trailing their continents of
shadow after them; and catching presently on an
intercepting peak, wrapped it about and brooded
there — then shredded away again and left the
purple peak, as they had left the purple domes,
downy and white with new-laid snow. In passing,
these monstrous rags of cloud hung low and swept
along right over the spectator's head, swinging their
tatters so nearly in his face that his impulse was to
shrink when they came closest. In the one place I

speak of, one could look below him upon a world
of diminishing crags and canyons leading down,
down, and away to a vague plain with a thread in it
which was a road, and bunches of feathers in it which
were trees, — a pretty picture sleeping in the sunlight — but with a darkness stealing over it and
glooming its features deeper and deeper under the
frown of a coming storm; and then, while no film or
shadow marred the noon brightness of his high
perch, he could watch the tempest break forth down
there and see the lightnings leap from crag to crag
and the sheeted rain drive along the canyon-sides,
and hear the thunders peal and crash and roar. We
had this spectacle; a familar one to many, but to
us a novelty.

We bowled along cheerily, and presently, at the
very summit (though it had been all summit to us,
and all equally level, for half an hour or more), we
came to a spring which spent its water through two
outlets and sent it in opposite directions. The conductor said that one of those streams which we were
looking at was just starting on a journey westward
to the Gulf of California and the Pacific Ocean,
through hundreds and even thousands of miles of
desert solitudes. He said that the other was just
leaving its home among the snow-peaks on a similar
journey eastward — and we knew that long after we
should have forgotten the simple rivulet it would still
be plodding its patient way down the mountain sides,
and canyon-beds, and between the banks of the Yel-

lowstone; and by and by would join the broad Missouri and flow through unknown plains and deserts
and unvisited wildernesses; and add a long and trou-
bled pilgrimage among snags and wrecks and sand-
bars; and enter the Mississippi, touch the wharves
of St. Louis, and still drift on, traversing shoals and
rocky channels, then endless chains of bottomless
and ample bends, walled with unbroken forests, then
mysterious byways and secret passages among
woody islands, then the chained bends again, bordered with wide levels of shining sugar-cane in place
of the sombre forests; then by New Orleans and still
other chains of bends — and finally, after two long
months of daily and nightly harassment, excitement,
enjoyment, adventure, and awful peril of parched
throats, pumps and evaporation, pass the Gulf and
enter into its rest upon the bosom of the tropic sea,
never to look upon its snow-peaks again or regret
them.

I freighted a leaf with a mental message for the
friends at home, and dropped it in the stream. But
I put no stamp on it and it was held for postage
somewhere.

On the summit we overtook an emigrant train of
many wagons, many tired men and women, and many
a disgusted sheep and cow. In the wofully dusty
horseman in charge of the expedition I recognized
John ———. Of all persons in the world to meet on
top of the Rocky Mountains thousands of miles from
home, he was the last one I should have looked for.

We were school-boys together and warm friends for
years. But a boyish prank of mine had disrup-
tured this friendship, and it had never been renewed.
The act of which I speak was this. I had been
accustomed to visit occasionally an editor whose
room was in the third story of a building and overlooked the street. One day this editor gave me a
watermelon which I made preparations to devour on
the spot, but chancing to look out of the window, I
saw John standing directly under it and an irresistible
desire came upon me to drop the melon on his head,
which I immediately did. I was the loser, for it
spoiled the melon, and John never forgave me, and
we dropped all intercourse and parted, but now met
again under these circumstances.

We recognized each other simultaneously, and
hands were grasped as warmly as if no coldness had
ever existed between us, and no allusion was made
to any. All animosities were buried, and the simple
fact of meeting a familiar face in that isolated spot
so far from home was sufficient to make us forget all
things but pleasant ones, and we parted again with
sincere " good-byes " and " God bless you " from
both.

We had been climbing up the long shoulders of
the Rocky Mountains for many tedious hours—we
started *down* them, now. And we went spinning
away at a round rate, too.

We left the snowy Wind River Mountains and the
Uinta Mountains behind, and sped away, always

through splendid scenery, but occasionally through
long ranks of white skeletons of mules and oxen —
monuments of the huge emigration of other days —
and here and there were up-ended boards or small
piles of stones which the driver said marked the rest-
ing-place of more precious remains. It was the
loneliest land for a grave! A land given over to the
cayote and the raven — which is but another name
for desolation and utter solitude. On damp, murky
nights, these scattered skeletons gave forth a soft,
hideous glow, like very faint spots of moonlight
starring the vague desert. It was because of the
phosphorus in the bones. But no scientific explanation could keep a body from shivering when he
drifted by one of those ghostly lights and knew
that a skull held it.

At midnight it began to rain, and I never saw anything like it — indeed, I did not even see this, for it
was too dark. We fastened down the curtains and
even caulked them with clothing, but the rain
streamed in in twenty places, notwithstanding.
There was no escape. If one moved his feet out of
a stream, he brought his body under one; and if he
moved his body he caught one somewhere else. If
he struggled out of the drenched blankets and sat
up, he was bound to get one down the back of his
neck. Meantime the stage was wandering about a
plain with gaping gullies in it, for the driver could
not see an inch before his face nor keep the road,
and the storm pelted so pitilessly that there was no

8

keeping the horses still. With the first abatement the conductor turned out with lanterns to look for the road, and the first dash he made was into a chasm about fourteen feet deep, his lantern following like a meteor. As soon as he touched bottom he sang out frantically:

"Don't come here!"

To which the driver, who was looking over the precipice where he had disappeared, replied, with an injured air: "Think I'm a dam fool?"

The conductor was more than an hour finding the road — a matter which showed us how far we had wandered and what chances we had been taking. He traced our wheel-tracks to the imminent verge of danger, in two places. I have always been glad that we were not killed that night. I do not know any particular reason, but I have always been glad.

In the morning, the tenth day out, we crossed Green River, a fine, large, limpid stream — stuck in it, with the water just up to the top of our mail-bed, and waited till extra teams were put on to haul us up the steep bank. But it was nice cool water, and besides it could not find any fresh place on us to wet.

At the Green River station we had breakfast — hot biscuits, fresh antelope steaks, and coffee — the only decent meal we tasted between the United States and Great Salt Lake City, and the only one we were ever really thankful for. Think of the monotonous execrableness of the thirty that went before it, to leave this one simple breakfast looming up

in my memory like a shot-tower after all these years
have gone by!

At five P.M. we reached Fort Bridger, one hundred and seventeen miles from the South Pass, and
one thousand and twenty-five miles from St. Joseph.
Fifty-two miles further on, near the head of Echo
Canyon, we met sixty United States soldiers from
Camp Floyd. The day before, they had fired upon
three hundred or four hundred Indians, whom they
supposed gathered together for no good purpose.
In the fight that had ensued, four Indians were captured, and the main body chased four miles, but
nobody killed. This looked like business. We had
a notion to get out and join the sixty soldiers, but
upon reflecting that there were four hundred of the
Indians, we concluded to go on and join the Indians.

Echo Canyon is twenty miles long. It was like a
long, smooth, narrow street, with a gradual descending grade, and shut in by enormous perpendicular
walls of coarse conglomerate, four hundred feet high
in many places, and turreted like mediæval castles.
This was the most faultless piece of road in the
mountains, and the driver said he would "let his
team out." He did, and if the Pacific express trains
whiz through there now any faster than we did then
in the stage-coach, I envy the passengers the exhilara-
tion of it. We fairly seemed to pick up our wheels
and fly — and the mail matter was lifted up free from
everything and held in solution! I am not given to
exaggeration, and when I say a thing I mean it.

However, time presses.   At four in the afternoon
we arrived on the summit of Big Mountain, fifteen
miles from Salt Lake City, when all the world was
glorified with the setting sun, and the most stupend-
ous panorama of mountain peaks yet encountered
burst on our sight.   We looked out upon this sublime spectacle from under the arch of a brilliant rain-
bow!   Even the Overland stage-driver stopped his
horses and gazed !

Half an hour or an hour later, we changed horses,
and took supper with a Mormon " Destroying
Angel."   " Destroying Angels," as I understand
it, are Latter-Day Saints who are set apart by the
Church to conduct permanent disappearances of ob-
noxious citizens.   I had heard a deal about these
Mormon Destroying Angels and the dark and bloody
deeds they had done, and when I entered this one's
house I had my shudder all ready.   But alas for all
our romances, he was nothing but a loud, profane,
offensive, old blackguard!   He was murderous
enough, possibly, to fill the bill of a Destroyer, but
would you have *any* kind of an Angel devoid of dignity?   Could you abide an Angel in an unclean shirt
and no suspenders?   Could you respect an Angel
with a horse-laugh and a swagger like a buccaneer?

There were other blackguards present — comrades of this one.   And there was one person that
looked like a gentleman — Heber C. Kimball's son,
tall and well made, and thirty years old, perhaps.
A lot of slatternly women flitted hither and thither in

a hurry, with coffee-pots, plates of bread, and other appurtenances to supper, and these were said to be the wives of the Angel — or some of them at least. And of course they were; for if they had been hired " help " they would not have let an angel from above storm and swear at them as he did, let alone one from the place this one hailed from.

This was our first experience of the Western " peculiar institution," and it was not very prepossessing. We did not tarry long to observe it, but hurried on to the home of the Latter-Day Saints, the stronghold of the prophets, the capital of the only absolute monarchy in America — Great Salt Lake City. As the night closed in we took sanctuary in the Salt Lake House and unpacked our baggage.

CHAPTER XIII.

WE had a fine supper, of the freshest meats and fowls and vegetables — a great variety and as great abundance. We walked about the streets some, afterward, and glanced in at shops and stores; and there was fascination in surreptitiously staring at every creature we took to be a Mormon. This was fairy-land to us, to all intents and purposes — a land of enchantment, and goblins, and awful mystery. We felt a curiosity to ask every child how many mothers it had, and if it could tell them apart; and we experienced a thrill every time a dwelling-house door opened and shut as we passed, disclosing a glimpse of human heads and backs and shoulders — for we so longed to have a good satisfying look at a Mormon family in all its comprehensive ampleness, disposed in the customary concentric rings of its home circle.

By and by the Acting Governor of the Territory introduced us to other " Gentiles," and we spent a sociable hour with them. " Gentiles " are people who are not Mormons. Our fellow-passenger, Bemis, took care of himself, during this part of the evening, and did not make an overpowering success of it, either, for he came into our room in the hotel about eleven o'clock, full of cheerfulness, and talking loosely, disjointedly, and indiscriminately, and every now and then tugging out a ragged word by the roots that had more hiccups than syllables in it. This, together with his hanging his coat on the floor on one side of a chair, and his vest on the floor on the other side, and piling his pants on the floor just in front of the same chair, and then contemplating the general result with superstitious awe, and finally pronouncing it " too many for *him* " and going to bed with his boots on, led us to fear that something he had eaten had not agreed with him.

But we knew afterward that it was something he had been drinking. It was the exclusively Mormon refresher, " valley tan." Valley tan (or, at least, one form of valley tan) is a kind of whisky, or first cousin to it; is of Mormon invention and manufactured only in Utah. Tradition says it is made of (imported) fire and brimstone. If I remember rightly, no public drinking saloons were allowed in the kingdom by Brigham Young, and no private drinking permitted among the faithful, except they confined themselves to " valley tan."

Next day we strolled about everywhere through the broad, straight, level streets, and enjoyed the pleasant strangeness of a city of fifteen thousand inhabitants with no loafers perceptible in it; and no visible drunkards or noisy people; a limpid stream

8.

rippling and dancing through every street in place of a filthy gutter; block after block of trim dwellings, built of " frame " and sunburned brick — a great thriving orchard and garden behind every one of them, apparently — branches from the street stream winding and sparkling among the garden beds and fruit trees — and a grand general air of neatness, repair, thrift, and comfort, around and about and over the whole. And everywhere were workshops, factories, and all manner of industries; and intent faces and busy hands were to be seen wherever one looked; and in one's ears was the ceaseless clink of hammers, the buzz of trade and the contented hum of drums and fly-wheels.

The armorial crest of my own State consisted of two dissolute bears holding up the head of a dead and gone cask between them and making the pertinent remark, " UNITED, WE STAND — (hic!) — DIVIDED, WE FALL." It was always too figurative for the author of this book. But the Mormon crest was easy. And it was simple, unostentatious, and fitted like a glove. It was a representation of a GOLDEN BEEHIVE, with the bees all at work!

The city lies in the edge of a level plain as broad as the State of Connecticut, and crouches close down to the ground under a curving wall of mighty mountains whose heads are hidden in the clouds, and whose shoulders bear relics of the snows of winter all the summer long. Seen from one of these dizzy heights, twelve or fifteen miles off, Great Salt Lake

City is toned down and diminished till it is suggestive of a child's toy-village reposing under the majestic protection of the Chinese wall.

On some of these mountains, to the southwest,
it had been raining every day for two weeks, but not
a drop had fallen in the city. And on hot days in
late spring and early autumn the citizens could quit
fanning and growling and go out and cool off by
looking at the luxury of a glorious snow-storm
going on in the mountains. They could enjoy it
at a distance, at those seasons, every day, though
no snow would fall in their streets, or anywhere near
them.

Salt Lake City was healthy — an extremely healthy
city. They declared that there was only one physi-
cian in the place and he was arrested every week regularly and held to answer under the vagrant act for
having "no visible means of support." They
always give you a good substantial article of truth in
Salt Lake, and good measure and good weight, too.
Very often, if you wished to weigh one of their airiest
little commonplace statements you would want the
hay scales.

We desired to visit the famous inland sea, the
American "Dead Sea," the great Salt Lake — seventeen miles, horseback, from the city — for we had
dreamed about it, and thought about it, and talked
about it, and yearned to see it, all the first part of
our trip; but now when it was only arm's length
away it had suddenly lost nearly every bit of its in-

H *

terest.   And so we put it off, in a sort of general
way, till next day — and that was the last we ever
thought of it.   We dined with some hospitable Gentiles; and visited the foundation of the prodigious
temple; and talked long with that shrewd Connecticut Yankee, Heber C. Kimball (since deceased), a
saint of high degree and a mighty man of commerce.
We saw the "Tithing-House," and the "Lion
House," and I do not know or remember how many
more church and government buildings of various
kinds and curious names.   We flitted hither and
thither and enjoyed every hour, and picked up a
great deal of useful information and entertaining
nonsense, and went to bed at night satisfied.

The second day, we made the acquaintance of Mr.
Street (since deceased) and put on white shirts and
went and paid a state visit to the king.   He seemed
a quiet, kindly, easy-mannered, dignified, self-pos-
sessed old gentleman of fifty-five or sixty, and had a
gentle craft in his eye that probably belonged there.
He was very simply dressed and was just taking off
a straw hat as we entered.   He talked about Utah,
and the Indians, and Nevada, and general American
matters and questions, with our secretary and certain government officials who came with us.   But he
never paid any attention to me, notwithstanding I
made several attempts to "draw him out" on fed-
eral politics and his high-handed attitude toward
Congress.   I thought some of the things I said
were rather fine.   But he merely looked around at

me, at distant intervals, something as I have seen a benignant old cat look around to see which kitten was meddling with her tail. By and by I subsided into an indignant silence, and so sat until the end, hot and flushed, and execrating him in my heart for an ignorant savage. But he was calm. His conversation with those gentlemen flowed on as sweetly and peacefully and musically as any summer brook. When the audience was ended and we were retiring from the presence, he put his hand on my head, beamed down on me in an admiring way and said to my brother:

"Ah — your child, I presume? Boy or girl?"

CHAPTER XIV.

MR. STREET was very busy with his telegraphic matters — and considering that he had eight or nine hundred miles of rugged, snowy, uninhabited mountains, and waterless, treeless, melancholy deserts to traverse with his wire, it was natural and needful that he should be as busy as possible. He could not go comfortably along and cut his poles by the roadside, either, but they had to be hauled by ox teams across those exhausting deserts — and it was two days' journey from water to water, in one or two of them. Mr. Street's contract was a vast work, every way one looked at it; and yet to comprehend what the vague words "eight hundred miles of rugged mountains and dismal deserts" mean, one must go over the ground in person — pen-and-ink descriptions cannot convey the dreary reality to the reader. And after all, Mr. S.'s mightiest difficulty turned out to be one which he had never taken into the account at all. Unto Mormons he had sub-let the hardest and heaviest half of his great undertaking, and all of a sudden they concluded that they were going to make little or nothing, and so they tran-

quilly threw their poles overboard in mountain or
desert, just as it happened when they took the
notion, and drove home and went about their customary business! They were under written contract
to Mr. Street, but they did not care anything for
that. They said they would "admire" to see a
"Gentile" force a Mormon to fulfil a losing contract in Utah! And they made themselves very
merry over the matter. Street said — for it was he
that told us these things:

"I was in dismay. I was under heavy bonds to
complete my contract in a given time, and this disaster looked very much like ruin. It was an astound-
ing thing; it was such a wholly unlooked-for difficulty, that I was entirely nonplussed. I am a business man — have always been a business man — do
not know anything *but* business — and so you can
imagine how like being struck by lightning it was to
find myself in a country where *written contracts
were worthless!* — that main security, that sheet-
anchor, that absolute necessity, of business. My
confidence left me. There was no use in making
new contracts — that was plain. I talked with first
one prominent citizen and then another. They all
sympathized with me, first rate, but they did not
know how to help me. But at last a Gentile said,
' Go to Brigham Young! — these small fry cannot
do you any good.' I did not think much of the
idea, for if the *law* could not help me, what could
an individual do who had not even anything to do

with either making the laws or executing them? He
might be a very good patriarch of a church and
preacher in its tabernacle, but something sterner
than religion and moral suasion was needed to handle
a hundred refractory, half-civilized sub-contractors.
But what was a man to do? I thought if Mr. Young
could not do anything else, he might probably be
able to give me some advice and a valuable hint or
two, and so I went straight to him and laid the
whole case before him. He said very little, but he
showed strong interest all the way through. He examined all the papers in detail, and whenever there
seemed anything like a hitch, either in the papers
or in my statement, he would go back and take up
the thread and follow it patiently out to an intelligent and satisfactory result. Then he made a list of
the contractors' names. Finally he said:

"'Mr. Street, this is all perfectly plain. These
contracts are strictly and legally drawn, and are
duly signed and certified. These men manifestly
entered into them with their eyes open. I see no
fault or flaw anywhere.'

"Then Mr. Young turned to a man waiting at the
other end of the room and said: 'Take this list of
names to So-and-so, and tell him to have these men
here at such-and-such an hour.'

"They were there, to the minute. So was I. Mr.
Young asked them a number of questions, and their
answers made my statement good. Then he said to
them:

" ' You signed these contracts and assumed these obligations of your own free will and accord?

" ' Yes.'

" ' Then carry them out to the letter, if it makes paupers of you!   Go!'

"And they *did* go, too!   They are strung across the deserts now, working like bees.   And I never hear a word out of them.   There is a batch of governors, and judges, and other officials here, shipped from Washington, and they maintain the semblance of a republican form of government — but the petrified truth is that Utah is an absolute monarchy and Brigham Young is king!"

Mr. Street was a fine man, and I believe his story. I knew him well during several years afterward in San Francisco.

Our stay in Salt Lake City amounted to only two days, and therefore we had no time to make the customary inquisition into the workings of polygamy and get up the usual statistics and deductions preparatory to calling the attention of the nation at large once more to the matter.   I had the will to do it.   With the gushing self-sufficiency of youth I was feverish to plunge in headlong and achieve a great reform here — until I saw the Mormon women. Then I was touched.   My heart was wiser than my head.   It warmed toward these poor, ungainly, and pathetically " homely " creatures, and as I turned to hide the generous moisture in my eyes, I said, " No — the man that marries one of them has done

an act of Christian charity which entitles him to the
kindly applause of mankind, not their harsh cen-
sure — and the man that marries sixty of them has
done a deed of open-handed generosity so sublime
that the nations should stand uncovered in his presence and worship in silence.''*

---

* For a brief sketch of Mormon history, and the noted Mountain
Meadow massacre, see Appendices A and B.

CHAPTER XV.

IT is a luscious country for thrilling evening stories about assassinations of intractable Gentiles. I cannot easily conceive of anything more cosy than the night in Salt Lake which we spent in a Gentile den, smoking pipes and listening to tales of how Burton galloped in among the pleading and defenseless "'Morisites" and shot them down, men and women, like so many dogs. And how Bill Hickman, a Destroying Angel, shot Drown and Arnold dead for bringing suit against him for a debt. And how Porter Rockwell did this and that dreadful thing. And how heedless people often come to Utah and make remarks about Brigham, or polygamy, or some other sacred matter, and the very next morning at daylight such parties are sure to be found lying up some back alley, contentedly waiting for the hearse. And the next most interesting thing is to sit and listen to these Gentiles talk about polygamy; and how some portly old frog of an elder, or a bishop, marries a girl — likes her, marries her sister — likes her, marries another sister — likes her, takes another — likes her, marries her mother — likes her, marries her

9

father, grandfather, great grandfather, and then comes back hungry and asks for more. And how the pert young thing of eleven will chance to be the favorite wife, and her own venerable grandmother have to rank away down toward D 4 in their mutual husband's esteem, and have to sleep in the kitchen, as like as not. And how this dreadful sort of thing, this hiving together in one foul nest of mother and daughters, and the making a young daughter superior to her own mother in rank and authority, are things which Mormon women submit to because their religion teaches them that the more wives a man has on earth, and the more children he rears, the higher the place they will all have in the world to come — and the warmer, maybe, though they do not seem to say anything about that.

According to these Gentile friends of ours, Brigham Young's harem contains twenty or thirty wives. They said that some of them had grown old and gone out of active service, but were comfortably housed and cared for in the hennery — or the Lion House, as it is strangely named. Along with each wife were her children — fifty altogether. The house was perfectly quiet and orderly, when the children were still. They all took their meals in one room, and a happy and homelike sight it was pronounced to be. None of our party got an opportunity to take dinner with Mr. Young, but a Gentile by the name of Johnson professed to have enjoyed a sociable breakfast in the Lion House. He gave a prepos-

terous account of the "calling of the roll," and other
preliminaries, and the carnage that ensued when the
buckwheat cakes came in.   But he embellished rather
too much.   He said that Mr. Young told him several smart sayings of certain of his "two-year-olds,"
observing with some pride that for many years he
had been the heaviest contributor in that line to one
of the Eastern magazines; and then he wanted to
show Mr. Johnson one of the pets that had said
the last good thing, but he could not find the child.
He searched the faces of the children in detail,
but could not decide which one it was.   Finally,
he gave it up with a sigh and said: "I thought
I would know the little cub again, but I don't."
Mr. Johnson said further, that Mr. Young observed
that life was a sad, sad thing — "because the joy
of every new marriage a man contracted was so
apt to be blighted by the inopportune funeral of
a less recent bride."   And Mr. Johnson said that
while he and Mr. Young were pleasantly conversing
in private, one of the Mrs. Youngs came in and demanded a breast-pin, remarking that she had found
out that he had been giving a breast-pin to No. 6,
and *she*, for one, did not propose to let this partial-
ity go on without making a satisfactory amount of
trouble about it.   Mr. Young reminded her that
there was a stranger present.   Mrs. Young said that
if the state of things inside the house was not agreeable to the stranger, he could find room outside.   Mr.
Young promised the breast-pin, and she went away.

But in a minute or two another Mrs. Young came
in and demanded a breast-pin. Mr. Young began a
remonstrance, but Mrs. Young cut him short. She
said No. 6 had got one, and No. 11 was promised
one, and it was "no use for him to try to impose on
her — she hoped she knew her rights." He gave
his promise, and she went. And presently three
Mrs. Youngs entered in a body and opened on their
husband a tempest of tears, abuse, and entreaty.
They had heard all about No. 6, No. 11, and No.
14. Three more breast-pins were promised. They
were hardly gone when nine more Mrs. Youngs filed
into the presence, and a new tempest burst forth and
raged round about the prophet and his guest. Nine
breast-pins were promised, and the weird sisters filed
out again. And in came eleven more, weeping and
wailing and gnashing their teeth. Eleven promised
breast-pins purchased peace once more.

"That is a specimen," said Mr. Young. "You
see how it is. You see what a life I lead. A man
can't be wise all the time. In a heedless moment I
gave my darling No. 6 — excuse my calling her thus,
as her other name has escaped me for the moment
— a breast-pin. It was only worth twenty-five dollars — that is, *apparently* that was its whole cost —
but its ultimate cost was inevitably bound to be a
good deal more. You yourself have seen it climb
up to six hundred and fifty dollars — and alas, even
that is not the end! For I have wives all over this
Territory of Utah. I have dozens of wives whose

numbers, even, I do not know without looking in the family Bible. They are scattered far and wide among the mountains and valleys of my realm. And, mark you, every solitary one of them will hear of this wretched breast-pin, and every last one of them will have one or die. No. 6's breast-pin will cost me twenty-five hundred dollars before I see the end of it. And these creatures will compare these pins together, and if one is a shade finer than the rest, they will all be thrown on my hands, and I will have to order a new lot to keep peace in the family. Sir, you probably did not know it, but all the time you were present with my children your every movement was watched by vigilant servitors of mine. If you had offered to give a child a dime, or a stick of candy, or any trifle of the kind, you would have been snatched out of the house instantly, provided it could be done before your gift left your hand. Otherwise it would be absolutely necessary for you to make an exactly similar gift to all my children — and knowing by experience the importance of the thing, I would have stood by and seen to it myself that you did it, and did it thoroughly. Once a gentleman gave one of my children a tin whistle — a veritable invention of Satan, sir, and one which I have an unspeakable horror of, and so would you if you had eighty or ninety children in your house. But the deed was done — the man escaped. I knew what the result was going to be, and I thirsted for vengeance. I ordered out a flock of Destroying Angels, and they hunted the man far into the fastnesses of the Nevada mountains. But they never caught him. I am not cruel, sir — I am not vindictive except when sorely outraged — but if I had caught him, sir, so help me Joseph Smith, I would have locked him into the nursery till the brats whistled him to death. By the slaughtered body of St. Parley Pratt (whom God assoil!) there was never anything on this earth like it! *I* knew who gave the whistle to the child, but I could not make those jealous mothers believe me. They believed *I* did it, and the result was just what any man of reflection could have foreseen: I had to order a hundred and ten whistles — I think we had a hundred and ten children in the house then, but some of them are off at college now — I had to order a hundred and ten of those shrieking things, and I wish I may never speak another word if we didn't have to talk on our fingers entirely, from that time forth until the children got tired of the whistles. And if ever another man gives a whistle to a child of mine and I get my hands on him, I will hang him higher than Haman! That is the word with the bark on it! Shade of Nephi! *You* don't know anything about married life. I am rich, and everybody knows it. I am benevolent, and everybody takes advantage of it. I have a strong fatherly instinct, and all the foundlings are foisted on me. Every time a woman wants to do well by her darling, she puzzles her brain to cipher out some scheme for getting it into my hands. Why, sir, a woman came here once with a

child of a curious lifeless sort of complexion (and so
had the woman), and swore that the child was mine
and she my wife — that I had married her at such-
and-such a time in such-and-such a place, but she had
forgotten her number, and of course I could not remember her name. Well, sir, she called my attention
to the fact that the child looked like me, and really
it did seem to resemble me — a common thing in the
Territory — and, to cut the story short, I put it in my
nursery, and she left. And, by the ghost of Orson
Hyde, when they came to wash the paint off that child
it was an Injun! Bless my soul, you don't know
anything about married life. It is a perfect dog's
life, sir — a perfect dog's life. You can't econo-
mize. It isn't possible. I have tried keeping one
set of bridal attire for all occasions. But it is of no
use. First you'll marry a combination of calico and
consumption that's as thin as a rail, and next you'll
get a creature that's nothing more than the dropsy in
disguise, and then you've got to eke out that bridal
dress with an old balloon. That is the way it goes.
And think of the wash-bill —(excuse these tears)
— nine hundred and eighty-four pieces a week!
No, sir, there is no such a thing as economy in a
family like mine. Why, just the one item of cradles
— think of it! And vermifuge! Soothing syrup!
Teething rings! And 'papa's watches' for the
babies to play with! And things to scratch the furniture with! And lucifer matches for them to eat,
and pieces of glass to cut themselves with! The item

9*

of glass alone would support *your* family, I venture
to say, sir.   Let me scrimp and squeeze all I can, I
still can't get ahead as fast as I feel I ought to, with
my opportunities.   Bless you, sir, at a time when I
had seventy-two wives in this house, I groaned under
the pressure of keeping thousands of dollars tied up
in seventy-two bedsteads when the money ought to
have been out at interest; and I just sold out the
whole stock, sir, at a sacrifice, and built a bedstead
seven feet long and ninety-six feet wide.   But it was
a failure, sir.   I could *not* sleep.   It appeared to me
that the whole seventy-two women snored at once.
The roar was deafening.   And then the danger of
it!   That was what I was looking at.   They would
all draw in their breath at once, and you could actually see the walls of the house suck in — and then
they would all exhale their breath at once, and you
could see the walls swell out, and strain, and hear
the rafters crack, and the shingles grind together.
My friend, take an old man's advice, and *don't* en-
cumber yourself with a large family— mind, I tell
you, don't do it.   In a small family, and in a small
family only, you will find that comfort and that peace
of mind which are the best at last of the blessings
this world is able to afford us, and for the lack of
which no accumulation of wealth, and no acquisition
of fame, power, and greatness can ever compensate
us.   Take my word for it, ten or eleven wives is all
you need — never go over it.''

Some instinct or other made me set this Johnson

down as being unreliable. And yet he was a very entertaining person, and I doubt if some of the information he gave us could have been acquired from any other source. He was a pleasant contrast to those reticent Mormons.

CHAPTER XVI.

ALL men have heard of the Mormon Bible, but few except the "elect" have seen it, or, at least, taken the trouble to read it. I brought away a copy from Salt Lake. The book is a curiosity to me, it is such a pretentious affair, and yet so "slow," so sleepy; such an insipid mess of inspiration. It is chloroform in print. If Joseph Smith composed this book, the act was a miracle — keeping awake while he did it was, at any rate. If he, according to tradition, merely translated it from certain ancient and mysteriously-engraved plates of copper, which he declares he found under a stone, in an out-of-the-way locality, the work of translating was equally a miracle, for the same reason.

The book seems to be merely a prosy detail of imaginary history, with the Old Testament for a model; followed by a tedious plagiarism of the New Testament. The author labored to give his words and phrases the quaint, old-fashioned sound and structure of our King James's translation of the Scriptures; and the result is a mongrel — half modern glibness, and half ancient simplicity and gravity.

(132)

The latter is awkward and constrained; the former natural, but grotesque by the contrast. Whenever he found his speech growing too modern — which was about every sentence or two — he ladled in a few such Scriptural phrases as "exceeding sore," "and it came to pass," etc., and made things satisfactory again. "And it came to pass" was his pet. If he had left that out, his Bible would have been only a pamphlet.

The title-page reads as follows:

THE BOOK OF MORMON: AN ACCOUNT WRITTEN BY THE HAND OF MORMON, UPON PLATES TAKEN FROM THE PLATES OF NEPHI.

Wherefore it is an abridgment of the record of the people of Nephi, and also of the Lamanites; written to the Lamanites, who are a remnant of the House of Israel; and also to Jew and Gentile; written by way of commandment, and also by the spirit of prophecy and of revelation. Written and sealed up, and hid up unto the Lord, that they might not be destroyed; to come forth by the gift and power of God unto the interpretation thereof; sealed by the hand of Moroni, and hid up unto the Lord, to come forth in due time by the way of Gentile; the interpretation thereof by the gift of God. An abridgment taken from the Book of Ether also; which is a record of the people of Jared; who were scattered at the time the Lord confounded the language of the people when they were building a tower to get to Heaven.

"Hid up" is good. And so is "wherefore" — though why "wherefore"? Any other word would have answered as well — though in truth it would not have sounded so Scriptural.

Next comes

THE TESTIMONY OF THREE WITNESSES.

Be it known unto all nations, kindreds, tongues, and people unto whom this work shall come, that we, through the grace of God the

Father, and our Lord Jesus Christ, have seen the plates which contain this record, which is a record of the people of Nephi, and also of the Lamanites, their brethren, and also of the people of Jared, who came from the tower of which hath been spoken; and we also know that they have been translated by the gift and power of God, for His voice hath declared it unto us; wherefore we know of a surety that the work is true. And we also testify that we have seen the engravings which are upon the plates; and they have been shown unto us by the power of God, and not of man.   And we declare with words of soberness, that an angel of God came down from heaven, and he brought and laid before our eyes, that we beheld and saw the plates, and the engravings thereon; and we know that it is by the grace of God the Father, and our Lord Jesus Christ, that we beheld and bear record that these things are true; and it is marvelous in our eyes; nevertheless the voice of the Lord commanded us that we should bear record of it; wherefore, to be obedient unto the commandments of God, we bear testimony of these things. And we know that if we are faithful in Christ, we shall rid our garments of the blood of all men, and be found spotless before the judgment-seat of Christ, and shall dwell with Him eternally in the heavens.   And the honor be to the Father, and to the Son, and to the Holy Ghost, which is one God.   Amen.

OLIVER COWDERY,
DAVID WHITMER,
MARTIN HARRIS.

Some people have to have a world of evidence before they can come anywhere in the neighborhood of believing anything; but for me, when a man tells me that he has " seen the engravings which are upon the plates," and not only that, but an angel was there at the time, and saw him see them, and probably took his receipt for it, I am very far on the road to conviction, no matter whether I ever heard of that man before or not, and even if I do not know the name of the angel, or his nationality either.

Next is this:

AND ALSO THE TESTIMONY OF EIGHT WITNESSES.

Be it known unto all nations, kindreds, tongues, and people unto whom this work shall come, that Joseph Smith, Jr., the translator of this work, has shown unto us the plates of which hath been spoken, which have the appearance of gold; and as many of the leaves as the said Smith has translated, we did handle with our hands; and we also saw the engravings thereon, all of which has the appearance of ancient work, and of curious workmanship. And this we bear record with words of soberness, that the said Smith has shown unto us, for we have seen and hefted, and know of a surety that the said Smith has got the plates of which we have spoken. And we give our names unto the world, to witness unto the world that which we have seen; and we lie not, God bearing witness of it.

CHRISTIAN WHITMER,	HIRAM PAGE,
JACOB WHITMER,	JOSEPH SMITH, SR.,
PETER WHITMER, JR.,	HYRUM SMITH,
JOHN WHITMER,	SAMUEL H. SMITH.

And when I am far on the road to conviction, and eight men, be they grammatical or otherwise, come forward and tell me that they have seen the plates too; and not only seen those plates but " hefted " them, I *am* convinced. I could not feel more satisfied and at rest if the entire Whitmer family had testified.

The Mormon Bible consists of fifteen " books " — being the books of Jacob, Enos, Jarom, Omni, Mosiah, Zeniff, Alma, Helaman, Ether, Moroni, two " books " of Mormon, and three of Nephi.

In the first book of Nephi is a plagiarism of the Old Testament, which gives an account of the exodus from Jerusalem of the " children of Lehi "; and it goes on to tell of their wanderings in the wilderness, during eight years, and their supernatural pro-

tection by one of their number, a party by the name
of Nephi.   They finally reached the land of " Boun-
tiful," and camped by the sea.   After they had remained there " for the space of many days " —
which is more Scriptural than definite — Nephi was
commanded from on high to build a ship wherein to
" carry the people across the waters."   He traves-
tied Noah's ark — but he obeyed orders in the matter of the plan.   He finished the ship *in a single
day*, while his brethren stood by and made fun of it
— and of him, too —" saying, our brother is a fool,
for he thinketh that he can build a ship."   They did
not wait for the timbers to dry, but the whole tribe
or nation sailed the next day.   Then a bit of genuine
nature cropped out, and is revealed by outspoken
Nephi with Scriptural frankness — they all got on a
spree !   They, " and also their wives, began to make
themselves merry, insomuch that they began to dance,
and to sing, and to speak with much rudeness; yea,
they were lifted up unto exceeding rudeness."

Nephi tried to stop these scandalous proceedings;
but they tied him neck and heels, and went on with
their lark.   But observe how Nephi the prophet cir-
cumvented them by the aid of the invisible powers:

And it came to pass that after they had bound me, insomuch that I
could not move, the compass, which had been prepared of the Lord,
did cease to work ; wherefore, they knew not whither they should steer
the ship, insomuch that there arose a great storm, yea, a great and terrible tempest, and we were driven back upon the waters for the space of
three days ; and they began to be frightened exceedingly, lest they
should be drowned in the sea ; nevertheless they did not loose me. And

on the fourth day, which we had been driven back, the tempest began to be exceeding sore.

And it came to pass that we were about to be swallowed up in the depths of the sea.

Then they untied him.

And it came to pass after they had loosed me, behold, I took the compass, and it did work whither I desired it. And it came to pass that I prayed unto the Lord ; and after I had prayed, the winds did cease, and the storm did cease, and there was a great calm.

Equipped with their compass, these ancients appear to have had the advantage of Noah.

Their voyage was toward a " promised land " — the only name they gave it. They reached it in safety.

Polygamy is a recent feature in the Mormon religion, and was added by Brigham Young after Joseph Smith's death. Before that, it was regarded as an " abomination." This verse from the Mormon Bible occurs in Chapter II of the book of Jacob:

For behold, thus saith the Lord, this people begin to wax in iniquity ; they understand not the Scriptures ; for they seek to excuse themselves in committing whoredoms, because of the things which were written concerning David, and Solomon his son. Behold, David and Solomon truly had many wives and concubines, which thing was abominable before me, saith the Lord ; wherefore, thus saith the Lord, I have led this people forth out of the land of Jerusalem, by the power of mine arm, that I might raise up unto me a righteous branch from the fruit of the loins of Joseph. Wherefore, I the Lord God, will not suffer that this people shall do like unto them of old.

However, the project failed — or at least the modern Mormon end of it — for Brigham " suffers " it. This verse is from the same chapter:

Behold, the Lamanites your brethren, whom you hate, because of their filthiness and the cursings which hath come upon their skins, are more righteous than you ; for they have not forgotten the commandment of the Lord, which was given unto our fathers, that they should have, save it were one wife ; and concubines they should have none.

The following verse (from Chapter IX of the Book of Nephi) appears to contain information not familiar to everybody :

And now it came to pass that when Jesus had ascended into heaven, the multitude did disperse, and every man did take his wife and his children, and did return to his own home.

And it came to pass that on the morrow, when the multitude was gathered together, behold, Nephi and his brother whom he had raised from the dead, whose name was Timothy, and also his son, whose name was Jonas, and also Mathoni, and Mathonihah, his brother, and Kumen, and Kumenonhi, and Jeremiah, and Shemnon, and Jonas, and Zedekiah, and Isaiah; now these were the names of the disciples whom Jesus had chosen.

In order that the reader may observe how much more grandeur and picturesqueness (as seen by these Mormon twelve) accompanied one of the tenderest episodes in the life of our Saviour than other eyes seem to have been aware of, I quote the following from the same " book " — Nephi :

And it came to pass that Jesus spake unto them, and bade them arise. And they arose from the earth, and He said unto them, Blessed are ye because of your faith. And now behold, My joy is full. And when He had said these words, He wept, and the multitude bear record of it, and He took their little children, one by one, and blessed them, and prayed unto the Father for them. And when He had done this He wept again, and He spake unto the multitude, and saith unto them, Behold your little ones. And as they looked to behold, they cast their eyes toward heaven, and they saw the heavens open, and they saw angels descending out of heaven as it were, in the midst of fire ; and

they came down and encircled those little ones about, and they were encircled about with fire ; and the angels did minister unto them, and the
multitude did see and hear and bear record ; and they know that their
record is true, for they all of them did see and hear, every man for himself ; and they were in number about two thousand and five hundred
souls ; and they did consist of men, women, and children.

And what else would they be likely to consist of?
The Book of Ether is an incomprehensible medley
of "history," much of it relating to battles and
sieges among peoples whom the reader has possibly
never heard of; and who inhabited a country which
is not set down in the geography. There was a
King with the remarkable name of Coriantumr, and
he warred with Shared, and Lib, and Shiz, and
others, in the "plains of Heshlon"; and the "valley of Gilgal"; and the "wilderness of Akish";
and the "land of Moran"; and the "plains of
Agosh"; and "Ogath," and "Ramah," and the
"land of Corihor," and the "hill Comnor," by
"the waters of Ripliancum," etc., etc., etc. "And
it came to pass," after a deal of fighting, that Coriantumr, upon making calculation of his losses, found
that "there had been slain two millions of mighty
men, and also their wives and their children" — say
5,000,000 or 6,000,000 in all — "and he began to
sorrow in his heart." Unquestionably it was time.
So he wrote to Shiz, asking a cessation of hostili-
ties, and offering to give up his kingdom to save
his people. Shiz declined, except upon condition
that Coriantumr would come and let him cut his
head off first — a thing which Coriantumr would not

10

do. Then there was more fighting for a season; then *four years* were devoted to gathering the forces for a final struggle — after which ensued a battle, which, I take it, is the most remarkable set forth in history,— except, perhaps, that of the Kilkenny cats, which it resembles in some respects. This is the account of the gathering and the battle:

7. And it came to pass that they did gather together all the people, upon all the face of the land, who had not been slain, save it was Ether. And it came to pass that Ether did behold all the doings of the people ; and he beheld that the people who were for Coriantumr, were gathered together to the army of Coriantumr ; and the people who were for Shiz, were gathered together to the army of Shiz ; wherefore they were for the space of four years gathering together the people, that they might get all who were upon the face of the land, and that they might receive all the strength which it was possible that they could receive. And it came to pass that when they were all gathered together, every one to the army which he would, with their wives and their children ; both men, women, and children being armed with weapons of war, having shields, and breast-plates, and head-plates, and being clothed after the manner of war, they did march forth one against another, to battle ; and they fought all that day, and conquered not. And it came to pass that when it was night they were weary, and retired to their camps ; and after they had retired to their camps, they took up a howling and a lamentation for the loss of the slain of their people; and so great were their cries, their howlings and lamentations, that it did rend the air exceedingly. And it came to pass that on the morrow they did go again to battle, and great and terrible was that day ; nevertheless they conquered not, and when the night came again, they did rend the air with their cries, and their howlings, and their mournings, for the loss of the slain of their people.

8. And it came to pass that Coriantumr wrote again an epistle unto Shiz, desiring that he would not come again to battle, but that he would take the kingdom, and spare the lives of the people. But behold, the Spirit of the Lord had ceased striving with them, and Satan had full power over the hearts of the people, for they were given up unto the

hardness of their hearts and the blindness of their minds, that they might be destroyed ; wherefore they went again to battle. And it came to pass that they fought all that day, and when the night came they slept upon their swords ; and on the morrow they fought even until the night came ; and when the night came they were drunken with anger, even as a man who is drunken with wine ; and they slept again upon their swords ; and on the morrow they fought again ; and when the night came they had all fallen by the sword save it were fifty and two of the people of Coriantumr, and sixty and nine of the people of Shiz. And it came to pass that they slept upon their swords that night, and on the morrow they fought again, and they contended in their mights with their swords, and with their shields, all that day ; and when the night came there were thirty and two of the people of Shiz, and twenty and seven of the people of Coriantumr.

9. And it came to pass that they ate and slept, and prepared for death on the morrow. And they were large and mighty men, as to the strength of men. And it came to pass that they fought for the space of three hours, and they fainted with the loss of blood. And it came to pass that when the men of Coriantumr had received sufficient strength, that they could walk, they were about to flee for their lives, but behold, Shiz arose, and also his men, and he swore in his wrath that he would slay Coriantumr, or he would perish by the sword ; wherefore he did pursue them, and on the morrow he did overtake them ; and they fought again with the sword. And it came to pass that when they had all fallen by the sword, save it were Coriantumr and Shiz, behold Shiz had fainted with loss of blood. And it came to pass that when Coriantumr had leaned upon his sword, that he rested a little, he smote off the head of Shiz. And it came to pass that after he had smote off the head of Shiz, that Shiz raised upon his hands and fell ; and after that he had struggled for breath, he died. And it came to pass that Coriantumr fell to the earth, and became as if he had no life. And the Lord spake unto Ether, and said unto him, go forth. And he went forth, and beheld that the words of the Lord had all been fulfilled ; and he finished his record ; and the hundredth part I have not written.

It seems a pity he did not finish, for after all his dreary former chapters of commonplace, he stopped just as he was in danger of becoming interesting.

The Mormon Bible is rather stupid and tiresome to read, but there is nothing vicious in its teachings. Its code of morals is unobjectionable — it is "smouched"* from the New Testament and no credit given.

---

* Milton.

CHAPTER XVII.

AT the end of our two days' sojourn, we left Great Salt Lake City hearty and well fed and happy — physically superb but not so very much wiser, as regards the "Mormon question," than we were when we arrived, perhaps. We had a deal more "information" than we had before, of course, but we did not know what portion of it was reliable and what was not — for it all came from acquaintances of a day — strangers, strictly speaking. We were told, for instance, that the dreadful "Mountain Meadows Massacre" was the work of the Indians entirely, and that the Gentiles had meanly tried to fasten it upon the Mormons; we were told, likewise, that the Indians were to blame, partly, and partly the Mormons; and we were told, likewise, and just as positively, that the Mormons were almost if not wholly and completely responsible for that most treacherous and pitiless butchery. We got the story in all these different shapes, but it was not till several years afterward that Mrs. Waite's book, "The Mormon Prophet," came out with Judge Cradlebaugh's trial of the accused parties in it

(143)

and revealed the truth that the latter version was the correct one and that the Mormons *were* the assassins. All our " information " had three sides to it, and so I gave up the idea that I could settle the " Mormon question " in two days. Still I have seen newspaper correspondents do it in one.

I left Great Salt Lake a good deal confused as to what state of things existed there — and sometimes even questioning in my own mind whether a state of things existed there at all or not. But presently I remembered with a lightening sense of relief that we had learned two or three trivial things there which we could be certain of; and so the two days were not wholly lost. For instance, we had learned that we were at last in a pioneer land, in absolute and tangible reality. The high prices charged for trifles were eloquent of high freights and bewildering distances of freightage. In the East, in those days, the smallest moneyed denomination was a penny and it represented the smallest purchasable quantity of any commodity. West of Cincinnati the smallest coin in use was the silver five-cent piece, and no smaller quantity of an article could be bought than " five cents' worth." In Overland City the lowest coin appeared to be the ten-cent piece; but in Salt Lake there did not seem to be any money in circulation smaller than a quarter, or any smaller quantity purchasable of any commodity than twenty-five cents' worth. We had always been used to half dimes and " five cents' worth " as the minimum of financial negotiations; but in Salt Lake if one wanted a cigar, it was a quarter; if he wanted a chalk pipe, it was a quarter; if he wanted a peach, or a candle, or a newspaper, or a shave, or a little Gentile whisky to rub on his corns to arrest indigestion and keep him from having the toothache, twenty-five cents was the price, every time. When we looked at the shot-bag of silver, now and then, we seemed to be wasting our substance in riotous living, but if we referred to the expense account we could see that we had not been doing anything of the kind. But people easily get reconciled to big money and big prices, and fond and vain of both — it is a descent to little coins and cheap prices that is hardest to bear and slowest to take hold upon one's toleration. After a month's acquaintance with the twenty-five cent minimum, the average human being is ready to blush every time he thinks of his despicable five-cent days. How sunburnt with blushes I used to get in gaudy Nevada, every time I thought of my first financial experience in Salt Lake. It was on this wise (which is a favorite expression of great authors, and a very neat one, too, but I never hear anybody *say* on this wise when they are talking). A young half-breed with a complexion like a yellow-jacket asked me if I would have my boots blacked. It was at the Salt Lake House the morning after we arrived. I said yes, and he blacked them. Then I handed him a silver five-cent piece, with the benevolent air of a person who is conferring wealth and blessedness upon poverty and

10*

suffering. The yellow-jacket took it with what I judged to be suppressed emotion, and laid it reverently down in the middle of his broad hand. Then he began to contemplate it, much as a philosopher contemplates a gnat's ear in the ample field of his microscope. Several mountaineers, teamsters, stage-drivers, etc., drew near and dropped into the tableau and fell to surveying the money with that attractive indifference to formality which is noticeable in the hardy pioneer. Presently the yellow-jacket handed the half dime back to me and told me I ought to keep my money in my pocket-book instead of in my soul, and then I wouldn't get it cramped and shriveled up so!

What a roar of vulgar laughter there was! I destroyed the mongrel reptile on the spot, but I smiled and smiled all the time I was detaching his scalp, for the remark he made *was* good for an " Injun."

Yes, we had learned in Salt Lake to be charged great prices without letting the inward shudder appear on the surface — for even already we had overheard and noted the tenor of conversations among drivers, conductors, and hostlers, and finally among citizens of Salt Lake, until we were well aware that these superior beings despised " emigrants." We permitted no tell-tale shudders and winces in our countenances, for we wanted to seem pioneers, or Mormons, half-breeds, teamsters, stage-drivers, Mountain Meadow assassins — anything in the world that the plains and Utah respected and admired —

but we were wretchedly ashamed of being emigrants," and sorry enough that we had white shirts and could not swear in the presence of ladies without looking the other way.

And many a time in Nevada, afterwards, we had occasion to remember with humiliation that we were "emigrants," and consequently a low and inferior sort of creatures. Perhaps the reader has visited Utah, Nevada, or California, even in these latter days, and while communing with himself upon the sorrowful banishment of those countries from what he considers "the world," has had his wings clipped by finding that *he* is the one to be pitied, and that there are entire populations around him ready and willing to do it for him — yea, who are complacently doing it for him already, wherever he steps his foot. Poor thing! they are making fun of his hat; and the cut of his New York coat; and his conscientiousness about his grammar; and his feeble profanity; and his consumingly ludicrous ignorance of ores, shafts, tunnels, and other things which he never saw before, and never felt enough interest in to read about. And all the time that he is thinking what a sad fate it is to be exiled to that far country, that lonely land, the citizens around him are looking down on him with a blighting compassion because he is an "emigrant" instead of that proudest and blessedest creature that exists on all the earth, a "FORTY-NINER."

The accustomed coach life began again, now, and

J*

by midnight it almost seemed as if we never had been out of our snuggery among the mail sacks at all. We had made one alteration, however. We had provided enough bread, boiled ham, and hard boiled eggs to last double the six hundred miles of staging we had still to do.

And it was comfort in those succeeding days to sit up and contemplate the majestic panorama of mountains and valleys spread out below us and eat ham and hard-boiled eggs while our spiritual natures reveled alternately in rainbows, thunderstorms, and peerless sunsets. Nothing helps scenery like ham and eggs. Ham and eggs, and after these a pipe — an old, rank, delicious pipe — ham and eggs and scenery, a " down grade," a flying coach, a fragrant pipe and a contented heart — these make happiness. It is what all the ages have struggled for.

CHAPTER XVIII.

AT eight in the morning we reached the remnant and ruin of what had been the important military station of "Camp Floyd," some forty-five or fifty miles from Salt Lake City. At four P.M. we had doubled our distance and were ninety or a hundred miles from Salt Lake. And now we entered upon one of that species of deserts whose concentrated hideousness shames the diffused and diluted horrors of Sahara — an "*alkali*" desert. For sixty-eight miles there was but one break in it. I do not remember that this was really a break; indeed, it seems to me that it was nothing but a watering depot *in the midst* of the stretch of sixty-eight miles. If my memory serves me, there was no well or spring at this place, but the water was hauled there by mule and ox teams from the further side of the desert. There was a stage station there. It was forty-five miles from the beginning of the desert, and twenty-three from the end of it.

We plowed and dragged and groped along, the whole livelong night, and at the end of this uncomfortable twelve hours we finished the forty-five-mile part of the desert and got to the stage station where the imported water was. The sun was just rising. It was easy enough to cross a desert in the night while we were asleep; and it was pleasant to reflect, in the morning, that we in actual person *had* encountered an absolute desert and could always speak knowingly of deserts in presence of the ignorant thenceforward. And it was pleasant also to reflect that this was not an obscure, back country desert, but a very celebrated one, the metropolis itself, as you may say. All this was very well and very comfortable and satisfactory — but now we were to cross a desert in *daylight*. This was fine — novel — romantic — dramatically adventurous — *this*, indeed, was worth living for, worth traveling for! We would write home all about it.

This enthusiasm, this stern thirst for adventure, wilted under the sultry August sun and did not last above one hour. One poor little hour — and then we were ashamed that we had "gushed" so. The poetry was all in the anticipation — there is none in the reality. Imagine a vast, waveless ocean stricken dead and turned to ashes; imagine this solemn waste tufted with ash-dusted sage-bushes; imagine the lifeless silence and solitude that belong to such a place; imagine a coach, creeping like a bug through the midst of this shoreless level, and sending up tumbled volumes of dust as if it were a bug that went by steam; imagine this aching monotony of toiling and plowing kept up hour after hour, and the shore

still as far away as ever, apparently; imagine team,
driver, coach and passengers so deeply coated with
ashes that they are all one colorless color; imagine
ash-drifts roosting above mustaches and eyebrows
like snow accumulations on boughs and bushes.
This is the reality of it.

The sun beats down with dead, blistering, relentless malignity; the perspiration is welling from every
pore in man and beast, but scarcely a sign of it finds
its way to the surface — it is absorbed before it gets
there; there is not the faintest breath of air stirring;
there is not a merciful shred of cloud in all the brilliant firmament; there is not a living creature visible
in any direction whither one searches the blank level
that stretches its monotonous miles on every hand;
there is not a sound — not a sigh — not a whisper —
not a buzz, or a whir of wings, or distant pipe of
bird — not even a sob from the lost souls that doubtless people that dead air. And so the occasional
sneezing of the resting mules and the champing of
the bits, grate harshly on the grim stillness, not dis-
sipating the spell but accenting it and making one
feel more lonesome and forsaken than before.

The mules, under violent swearing, coaxing, and
whip-cracking, would make at stated intervals a
" spurt," and drag the coach a hundred or may be
two hundred yards, stirring up a billowy cloud of
dust that rolled back, enveloping the vehicle to the
wheel-tops or higher, and making it seem afloat in a
fog. Then a rest followed, with the usual sneezing

and bit-champing.   Then another "spurt" of a
hundred yards and another rest at the end of it.
All day long we kept this up, without water for the
mules and without ever changing the team.   At least
we kept it up ten hours, which, I take it, is a day,
and a pretty honest one, in an alkali desert.   It was
from four in the morning till two in the afternoon.
And it was so hot! and so close! and our water
canteens went dry in the middle of the day and we
got so thirsty!   It was so stupid and tiresome and
dull! and the tedious hours did lag and drag and
limp along with such a cruel deliberation!   It was
so trying to give one's watch a good long undisturbed spell and then take it out and find that it had
been fooling away the time and not trying to get
ahead any!   The alkali dust cut through our lips, it
persecuted our eyes, it ate through the delicate
membranes and made our noses bleed and *kept* them
bleeding — and truly and seriously the romance all
faded far away and disappeared, and left the desert
trip nothing but a harsh reality — a thirsty, sweltering, longing, hateful reality!

Two miles and a quarter an hour for ten hours —
that was what we accomplished.   It was hard to
bring the comprehension away down to such a snail-
pace as that, when we had been used to making
eight and ten miles an hour.   When we reached
the station on the farther verge of the desert, we
were glad, for the first time, that the dictionary was
along, because we never could have found language

to tell how glad we were, in any sort of dictionary but an unabridged one with pictures in it. But there could not have been found in a whole library of dictionaries language sufficient to tell how tired those mules were after their twenty-three-mile pull. To try to give the reader an idea of how *thirsty* they were, would be to " gild refined gold or paint the lily."

Somehow, now that it is there, the quotation does not seem to fit—but no matter, let it stay, anyhow. I think it is a graceful and attractive thing, and therefore have tried time and time again to work it in where it *would* fit, but could not succeed. These efforts have kept my mind distracted and ill at ease, and made my narrative seem broken and disjointed, in places. Under these circumstances it seems to me best to leave it in, as above, since this will afford at least a temporary respite from the wear and tear of trying to " lead up " to this really apt and beautiful quotation.

CHAPTER XIX.

ON the morning of the sixteenth day out from St. Joseph we arrived at the entrance of Rocky Canyon, two hundred and fifty miles from Salt Lake. It was along in this wild country somewhere, and far from any habitation of white men, except the stage stations, that we came across the wretchedest type of mankind I have ever seen, up to this writing. I refer to the Goshoot Indians. From what we could see and all we could learn, they are very considerably inferior to even the despised Digger Indians of California; inferior to all races of savages on our continent; inferior to even the Terra del Fuegans; inferior to the Hottentots, and actually inferior in some respects to the Kytches of Africa. Indeed, I have been obliged to look the bulky volumes of Wood's " Uncivilized Races of Men " clear through in order to find a savage tribe degraded enough to take rank with the Goshoots. I find but one people fairly open to that shameful verdict. It is the Bosjesmans (Bushmen) of South Africa. Such of the Goshoots as we saw, along the road and hanging about the stations, were small, lean, "scrawny" creatures; in complexion a dull black like the ordinary American negro; their faces and hands bearing dirt which they had been hoarding and accumulating for months, years, and even generations, according to the age of the proprietor; a silent, sneaking, treacherous-looking race; taking note of everything, covertly, like all the other "Noble Red Men" that we (do not) read about, and betraying no sign in their countenances; indolent, everlastingly patient and tireless, like all other Indians; prideless beggars — for if the beggar instinct were left out of an Indian he would not "go," any more than a clock without a pendulum; hungry, always hungry, and yet never refusing anything that a hog would eat, though often eating what a hog would decline; hunters, but having no higher ambition than to kill and eat jackass rabbits, crickets, and grasshoppers, and embezzle carrion from the buzzards and cayotes; savages who, when asked if they have the common Indian belief in a Great Spirit show a something which almost amounts to emotion, thinking whisky is referred to; a thin, scattering race of almost naked black children, these Goshoots are, who produce nothing at all, and have no villages, and no gatherings together into strictly defined tribal communities — a people whose only shelter is a rag cast on a bush to keep off a portion of the snow, and yet who inhabit one of the most rocky, wintry, repulsive wastes that our country or any other can exhibit.

The Bushmen and our Goshoots are manifestly descended from the self-same gorilla, or kangaroo, or Norway rat, whichever animal-Adam the Darwinians trace them to.

One would as soon expect the rabbits to fight as the Goshoots, and yet they used to live off the offal and refuse of the stations a few months and then come some dark night when no mischief was expected, and burn down the buildings and kill the men from ambush as they rushed out. And once, in the night, they attacked the stage-coach when a District Judge, of Nevada Territory, was the only passenger, and with their first volley of arrows (and a bullet or two) they riddled the stage curtains, wounded a horse or two and mortally wounded the driver. The latter was full of pluck, and so was his passenger. At the driver's call Judge Mott swung himself out, clambered to the box and seized the reins of the team, and away they plunged, through the racing mob of skeletons and under a hurtling storm of missiles. The stricken driver had sunk down on the boot as soon as he was wounded, but had held on to the reins and said he would manage to keep hold of them until relieved. And after they were taken from his relaxing grasp, he lay with his head between Judge Mott's feet, and tranquilly gave directions about the road; he said he believed he could live till the miscreants were outrun and left behind, and that if he managed that, the main difficulty would be at an end, and then if the Judge drove so and so (giving directions about bad places in the road, and general course) he would reach the next station without trouble. The Judge distanced the enemy and at last rattled up to the station and knew that the night's perils were done; but there was no comrade-in-arms for him to rejoice with, for the soldierly driver was dead.

Let us forget that we have been saying harsh things about the Overland drivers, now. The disgust which the Goshoots gave me, a disciple of Cooper and a worshiper of the Red Man — even of the scholarly savages in the "Last of the Mohicans" who are fittingly associated with backwoodsmen who divide each sentence into two equal parts; one part critically grammatical, refined, and choice of language, and the other part just such an attempt to talk like a hunter or a mountaineer as a Broadway clerk might make after eating an edition of Emerson Bennett's works and studying frontier life at the Bowery Theatre a couple of weeks — I say that the nausea which the Goshoots gave me, an Indian worshiper, set me to examining authorities, to see if perchance I had been over-estimating the Red Man while viewing him through the mellow moonshine of romance. The revelations that came were disenchanting. It was curious to see how quickly the paint and tinsel fell away from him and left him treacherous, filthy, and repulsive — and how quickly the evidences accumulated that wherever one finds an Indian tribe he has only found Goshoots more

or less modified by circumstances and surroundings — but Goshoots, after all. They deserve pity,
poor creatures! and they can have mine — at this
distance. Nearer by, they never get anybody's.

There is an impression abroad that the Baltimore
and Washington Railroad Company and many of its
employes are Goshoots; but it is an error. There
is only a plausible resemblance, which, while it is
apt enough to mislead the ignorant, cannot deceive
parties who have contemplated both tribes. But
seriously, it was not only poor wit, but very wrong
to start the report referred to above; for however
innocent the motive may have been, the necessary
effect was to injure the reputation of a class who
have a hard enough time of it in the pitiless deserts
of the Rocky Mountains, Heaven knows! If we
cannot find it in our hearts to give those poor naked
creatures our Christian sympathy and compassion, in
God's name let us at least not throw mud at them.

CHAPTER XX.

ON the seventeenth day we passed the highest mountain peaks we had yet seen, and although the day was very warm the night that followed upon its heels was wintry cold and blankets were next to useless.

On the eighteenth day we encountered the eastward-bound telegraph-constructors at Reese River station and sent a message to his Excellency Gov. Nye at Carson City (distant one hundred and fifty-six miles).

On the nineteenth day we crossed the Great American Desert — forty memorable miles of bottomless sand, into which the coach wheels sunk from six inches to a foot. We worked our passage most of the way across. That is to say, we got out and walked. It was a dreary pull and a long and thirsty one, for we had no water. From one extremity of this desert to the other, the road was white with the bones of oxen and horses. It would hardly be an exaggeration to say that we could have walked the forty miles and set our feet on a bone at every step! The desert was one prodigious grave-

yard.   And the log-chains, wagon tires, and rot-
ting wrecks of vehicles were almost as thick as the
bones.   I think we saw log-chains enough rusting
there in the desert to reach across any State in the
Union.   Do not these relics suggest something of
an idea of the fearful suffering and privation the
early emigrants to California endured?

At the border of the desert lies Carson Lake, or
the "Sink" of the Carson, a shallow, melancholy
sheet of water some eighty or a hundred miles in
circumference.   Carson River empties into it and
is lost — sinks mysteriously into the earth and never
appears in the light of the sun again — for the lake
has no outlet whatever.

There are several rivers in Nevada, and they all
have this mysterious fate.   They end in various
lakes or "sinks," and that is the last of them.
Carson Lake, Humboldt Lake, Walker Lake, Mono
Lake, are all great sheets of water without any
visible outlet.   Water is always flowing into them;
none is ever seen to flow out of them, and yet they
remain always level full, neither receding nor over-
flowing.   What they do with their surplus is only
known to the Creator.

On the western verge of the desert we halted a
moment at Ragtown.   It consisted of one log-house
and is not set down on the map.

This reminds me of a circumstance.   Just after
we left Julesburg, on the Platte, I was sitting with
the driver, and he said:

"I can tell you a most laughable thing indeed, if you would like to listen to it. Horace Greeley went over this road once. When he was leaving Carson City he told the driver, Hank Monk, that he had an engagement to lecture at Placerville and was very anxious to go through quick. Hank Monk cracked his whip and started off at an awful pace. The coach bounced up and down in such a terrific way that it jolted the buttons all off of Horace's coat, and finally shot his head clean through the roof of the stage, and then he yelled at Hank Monk and begged him to go easier — said he warn't in as much of a hurry as he was awhile ago. But Hank Monk said, 'Keep your seat, Horace, and I'll get you there on time' — and you bet you he did, too, what was left of him!"

A day or two after that we picked up a Denver man at the cross roads, and he told us a good deal about the country and the Gregory Diggings. He seemed a very entertaining person and a man well posted in the affairs of Colorado. By and by he remarked:

"I can tell you a most laughable thing indeed, if you would like to listen to it. Horace Greeley went over this road once. When he was leaving Carson City he told the driver, Hank Monk, that he had an engagement to lecture at Placerville and was very anxious to go through quick. Hank Monk cracked his whip and started off at an awful pace. The coach bounced up and down in such a terrific

11.

way that it jolted the buttons all off of Horace's coat, and finally shot his head clean through the roof of the stage, and then he yelled at Hank Monk and begged him to go easier — said he warn't in as much of a hurry as he was awhile ago. But Hank Monk said, 'Keep your seat, Horace, and I'll get you there on time !' — and you bet you he did, too, what was left of him !''

At Fort Bridger, some days after this, we took on board a cavalry sergeant, a very proper and soldierly person indeed. From no other man during the whole journey did we gather such a store of concise and well-arranged military information. It was surprising to find in the desolate wilds of our country a man so thoroughly acquainted with everything useful to know in his line of life, and yet of such inferior rank and unpretentious bearing. For as much as three hours we listened to him with unabated interest. Finally he got upon the subject of trans-continental travel, and presently said :

'' I can tell you a very laughable thing indeed, if you would like to listen to it. Horace Greeley went over this road once. When he was leaving Carson City he told the driver, Hank Monk, that he had an engagement to lecture at Placerville and was very anxious to go through quick. Hank Monk cracked his whip and started off at an awful pace. The coach bounced up and down in such a terrific way that it jolted the buttons all off of Horace's coat, and finally shot his head clean through the roof of the stage, and then he yelled at Hank Monk and begged him to go easier — said he warn't in as much of a hurry as he was awhile ago. But Hank Monk said, ' Keep your seat, Horace, and I'll get you there on time!' — and you bet you he did, too, what was left of him!''

When we were eight hours out from Salt Lake City a Mormon preacher got in with us at a way station — a gentle, soft-spoken, kindly man, and one whom any stranger would warm to at first sight. I can never forget the pathos that was in his voice as he told, in simple language, the story of his people's wanderings and unpitied sufferings. No pulpit eloquence was ever so moving and so beautiful as this outcast's picture of the first Mormon pilgrimage across the plains, struggling sorrowfully onward to the land of its banishment and marking its desolate way with graves and watering it with tears. His words so wrought upon us that it was a relief to us all when the conversation drifted into a more cheerful channel and the natural features of the curious country we were in came under treatment. One matter after another was pleasantly discussed, and at length the stranger said :

" I can tell you a most laughable thing indeed, if you would like to listen to it. Horace Greeley went over this road once. When he was leaving Carson City he told the driver, Hank Monk, that he had an engagement to lecture in Placerville, and was very anxious to go through quick. Hank

K.

Monk cracked his whip and started off at an awful
pace. The coach bounced up and down in such a
terrific way that it jolted the buttons all off of
Horace's coat, and finally shot his head clean
through the roof of the stage, and then he yelled at
Hank Monk and begged him to go easier — said he
warn't in as much of a hurry as he was awhile ago.
But Hank Monk said, 'Keep your seat, Horace,
and I'll get you there on time!'— and you bet you
he did, too, what was left of him!''

Ten miles out of Ragtown we found a poor
wanderer who had lain down to die. He had
walked as long as he could, but his limbs had failed
him at last. Hunger and fatigue had conquered
him. It would have been inhuman to leave him
there. We paid his fare to Carson and lifted him
into the coach. It was some little time before he
showed any very decided signs of life; but by dint
of chafing him and pouring brandy between his lips
we finally brought him to a languid consciousness.
Then we fed him a little, and by and by he seemed
to comprehend the situation and a grateful light
softened his eye. We made his mail-sack bed as
comfortable as possible, and constructed a pillow
for him with our coats. He seemed very thankful.
Then he looked up in our faces, and said in a
feeble voice that had a tremble of honest emotion
in it:

"Gentlemen, I know not who you are, but you
have saved my life; and although I can never be

able to repay you for it, I feel that I can at least make one hour of your long journey lighter. I take it you are strangers to this great thoroughfare, but I am entirely familiar with it. In this connection I can tell you a most laughable thing indeed, if you would like to listen to it. Horace Greeley —"

I said, impressively:

" Suffering stranger, proceed at your peril. You see in me the melancholy wreck of a once stalwart and magnificent manhood. What has brought me to this? That thing which you are about to tell. Gradually, but surely, that tiresome old anecdote has sapped my strength, undermined my constitution, withered my life. Pity my helplessness. Spare me only just this once, and tell me about young George Washington and his little hatchet for a change."

We were saved. But not so the invalid. In trying to retain the anecdote in his system he strained himself and died in our arms.

I am aware, now, that I ought not to have asked of the sturdiest citizen of all that region, what I asked of that mere shadow of a man; for, after seven years' residence on the Pacific coast, I know that no passenger or driver on the Overland ever corked that anecdote in, when a stranger was by, and survived. Within a period of six years I crossed and recrossed the Sierras between Nevada and California thirteen times by stage and listened to that deathless incident four hundred and eighty-one or eighty-two times. I have the list some-

where.   Drivers always told it, conductors told it,
landlords told it, chance passengers told it, the very
Chinamen and vagrant Indians recounted it.   I have
had the same driver tell it to me two or three times
in the same afternoon.   It has come to me in all
the multitude of tongues that Babel bequeathed to
earth, and flavored with whisky, brandy, beer,
cologne, sozodont, tobacco, garlic, onions, grasshoppers — everything that has a fragrance to it
through all the long list of things that are gorged or
guzzled by the sons of men.   I never have smelt
any anecdote as often as I have smelt that one;
never have smelt any anecdote that smelt so
variegated as that one.   And you never could learn
to know it by its smell, because every time you
thought you had learned the smell of it, it would
turn up with a different smell.   Bayard Taylor has
written about this hoary anecdote, Richardson has
published it; so have Jones, Smith, Johnson, Ross
Browne, and every other correspondence-inditing
being that ever set his foot upon the great overland
road anywhere between Julesburg and San Francisco; and I have heard that it is in the Talmud.   I
have seen it in print in nine different foreign lan-
guages; I have been told that it is employed in the
inquisition in Rome; and I now learn with regret
that it is going to be set to music.   I do not think
that such things are right.

Stage-coaching on the Overland is no more, and
stage drivers are a race defunct.   I wonder if they

bequeathed that bald-headed anecdote to their suc-
cessors, the railroad brakemen and conductors, and
if these latter still persecute the helpless passenger
with it until he concludes, as did many a tourist of
other days, that the real grandeurs of the Pacific
coast are not Yo Semite and the Big Trees, but
Hank Monk and his adventure with Horace
Greeley.*

---

* And what makes that worn anecdote the more aggravating, is, that
the adventure it celebrates *never occurred.* If it were a good anecdote,
that seeming demerit would be its chiefest virtue, for creative power be-
longs to greatness ; but what ought to be done to a man who would
wantonly contrive so flat a one as this ? If *I* were to suggest what
ought to be done to him, I should be called extravagant—but what does
the sixteenth chapter of Daniel say ?   Aha !

CHAPTER XXI.

WE were approaching the end of our long journey. It was the morning of the twentieth day. At noon we would reach Carson City, the capital of Nevada Territory. We were not glad, but sorry. It had been a fine pleasure trip; we had fed fat on wonders every day; we were now well accustomed to stage life, and very fond of it; so the idea of coming to a standstill and settling down to a humdrum existence in a village was not agreeable, **but** on the contrary depressing.

Visibly our new home was a desert, walled in by barren, snow-clad mountains. There was not a tree in sight. There was no vegetation but the endless sage-brush and greasewood. All nature was gray with it. We were ploughing through great deeps of powdery alkali dust that rose in thick clouds and floated across the plain like smoke from a burning house. We were coated with it like millers; so were the coach, the mules, the mail-bags, the driver — we and the sage-brush and the other scenery were all one monotonous color. Long trains of freight wagons in the distance enveloped in ascending masses of dust suggested pictures of prairies on fire. These teams and their masters were the only life we saw. Otherwise we moved in the midst of solitude, silence, and desolation. Every twenty steps we passed the skeleton of some dead beast of burthen, with its dust-coated skin stretched tightly over its empty ribs. Frequently a solemn raven sat upon the skull or the hips and contemplated the passing coach with meditative serenity.

By and by Carson City was pointed out to us. It nestled in the edge of a great plain and was a sufficient number of miles away to look like an assemblage of mere white spots in the shadow of a grim range of mountains overlooking it, whose summits seemed lifted clear out of companionship and consciousness of earthly things.

We arrived, disembarked, and the stage went on. It was a "wooden" town; its population two thousand souls. The main street consisted of four or five blocks of little white frame stores which were too high to sit down on, but not too high for various other purposes; in fact, hardly high enough. They were packed close together, side by side, as if room were scarce in that mighty plain. The sidewalk was of boards that were more or less loose and inclined to rattle when walked upon. In the middle of the town, opposite the stores, was the "plaza" which is native to all towns beyond the Rocky Mountains — a large, unfenced, level vacancy, with a liberty pole in it, and very useful as a place for public auctions, horse trades, and mass meetings, and likewise for teamsters to camp in. Two other sides of the plaza were faced by stores, offices, and stables. The rest of Carson City was pretty scattering.

We were introduced to several citizens, at the stage-office and on the way up to the Governor's from the hotel — among others, to a Mr. Harris, who was on horseback; he began to say something, but interrupted himself with the remark:

"I'll have to get you to excuse me a minute; yonder is the witness that swore I helped to rob the California coach — a piece of impertinent intermeddling, sir, for I am not even acquainted with the man."

Then he rode over and began to rebuke the stranger with a six-shooter, and the stranger began to explain with another. When the pistols were emptied, the stranger resumed his work (mending a whip-lash), and Mr. Harris rode by with a polite nod, homeward bound, with a bullet through one of his lungs, and several through his hips; and from them issued little rivulets of blood that coursed down the horse's sides and made the animal look quite picturesque. I never saw Harris shoot a man after that but it recalled to mind that first day in Carson.

This was all we saw that day, for it was two o'clock, now, and according to custom the daily "Washoe Zephyr" set in; a soaring dust-drift about the size of the United States set up edgewise came with it, and the capital of Nevada Territory disappeared from view. Still, there were sights to be seen which were not wholly uninteresting to new comers; for the vast dust cloud was thickly freckled with things strange to the upper air — things living and dead, that flitted hither and thither, going and coming, appearing and disappearing among the rolling billows of dust — hats, chickens, and parasols sailing in the remote heavens; blankets, tin signs, sage-brush, and shingles a shade lower; door-mats and buffalo robes lower still; shovels and coal scuttles on the next grade; glass doors, cats, and little children on the next; disrupted lumber yards, light buggies, and wheelbarrows on the next; and down only thirty or forty feet above ground was a scurrying storm of emigrating roofs and vacant lots.

It was something to see that much. I could have seen more, if I could have kept the dust out of my eyes.

But, seriously, a Washoe wind is by no means a trifling matter. It blows flimsy houses down, lifts shingle roofs occasionally, rolls up tin ones like sheet music, now and then blows a stage coach over and spills the passengers; and tradition says the reason there are so many bald people there, is, that the wind blows the hair off their heads while they are looking skyward after their hats. Carson streets seldom look inactive on summer afternoons, because there are so many citizens skipping around their escaping hats, like chambermaids trying to head off a spider.

The "Washoe Zephyr" (Washoe is a pet nick-

name for Nevada) is a peculiarly Scriptural wind, in
that no man knoweth "whence it cometh." That
is to say, where it *originates*. It comes right over
the mountains from the West, but when one crosses
the ridge he does not find any of it on the other
side! It probably is manufactured on the mountain
top for the occasion, and starts from there. It is a
pretty regular wind, in the summer time. Its office
hours are from two in the afternoon till two the next
morning; and anybody venturing abroad during
those twelve hours needs to allow for the wind or he
will bring up a mile or two to leeward of the point
he is aiming at. And yet the first complaint a
Washoe visitor to San Francisco makes, is that the
sea winds blow so, there! There is a good deal of
human nature in that.

We found the state palace of the Governor of
Nevada Territory to consist of a white frame one-
story house with two small rooms in it and a stanchion supported shed in front — for grandeur — it
compelled the respect of the citizen and inspired the
Indians with awe. The newly-arrived Chief and Asso-
ciate Justices of the Territory, and other machinery
of the government, were domiciled with less splendor.
They were boarding around privately, and had their
offices in their bedrooms.

The Secretary and I took quarters in the " ranch "
of a worthy French lady by the name of Bridget
O'Flannigan, a camp follower of his Excellency the
Governor. She had known him in his prosperity as

commander-in-chief of the Metropolitan Police of New York, and she would not desert him in his adversity as Governor of Nevada. Our room was on the lower floor, facing the plaza ; and when we had got our bed, a small table, two chairs, the government fire-proof safe, and the Unabridged Dictionary into it, there was still room enough left for a visitor — maybe two, but not without straining the walls. But the walls could stand it — at least the partitions could, for they consisted simply of one thickness of white "cotton domestic" stretched from corner to corner of the room. This was the rule in Carson — any other kind of partition was the rare exception. And if you stood in a dark room and your neighbors in the next had lights, the shadows on your canvas told queer secrets sometimes ! Very often these partitions were made of old flour sacks basted together; and then the difference between the common herd and the aristocracy was, that the common herd had unornamented sacks, while the walls of the aristocrat were overpowering with rudimental fresco — *i. e.*, red and blue mill brands on the flour sacks. Occasionally, also, the better classes embellished their canvas by pasting pictures from *Harper's Weekly* on them. In many cases, too, the wealthy and the cultured rose to spittoons and other evidences of a sumptuous and luxurious taste.* We

---

* Washoe people take a joke so hard that I must explain that the above description was only the rule ; there were many honorable exceptions in Carson — plastered ceilings and houses that had considerable furniture in them. — M. T.

had a carpet and a genuine queen's-ware washbowl. Consequently we were hated without reserve by the other tenants of the O'Flannigan "ranch." When we added a painted oilcloth window curtain, we simply took our lives into our own hands. To prevent bloodshed I removed up stairs and took up quarters with the untitled plebeians in one of the fourteen white pine cot-bedsteads that stood in two long ranks in the one sole room of which the second story consisted.

It was a jolly company, the fourteen. They were principally voluntary camp-followers of the Governor, who had joined his retinue by their own election at New York and San Francisco, and came along, feeling that in the scuffle for little territorial crumbs and offices they could not make their condition more precarious than it was, and might reasonably expect to make it better. They were popularly known as the "Irish Brigade," though there were only four or five Irishmen among all the Governor's retainers. His good-natured Excellency was much annoyed at the gossip his henchmen created — especially when there arose a rumor that they were paid assassins of his, brought along to quietly reduce the democratic vote when desirable!

Mrs. O'Flannigan was boarding and lodging them at ten dollars a week apiece, and they were cheerfully giving their notes for it. They were perfectly satisfied, but Bridget presently found that notes that could not be discounted were but a feeble constitution for a Carson boarding-house. So she began to harry the Governor to find employment for the "Brigade." Her importunities and theirs together drove him to a gentle desperation at last, and he finally summoned the Brigade to the presence. Then, said he:

"Gentlemen, I have planned a lucrative and useful service for you — a service which will provide you with recreation amid noble landscapes, and afford you never-ceasing opportunities for enriching your minds by observation and study. I want you to survey a railroad from Carson City westward to a certain point! When the legislature meets I will have the necessary bill passed and the remuneration arranged."

"What, a railroad over the Sierra Nevada Mountains?"

"Well, then, survey it eastward to a certain point!"

He converted them into surveyors, chain-bearers, and so on, and turned them loose in the desert. It was "recreation" with a vengeance! Recreation on foot, lugging chains through sand and sage-brush, under a sultry sun and among cattle bones, cayotes, and tarantulas. "Romantic adventure" could go no further. They surveyed very slowly, very deliberately, very carefully. They returned every night during the first week, dusty, footsore, tired, and hungry, but very jolly. They brought in great store of prodigious hairy spiders — tarantulas — and imprisoned them in covered tumblers up stairs in the

"ranch." After the first week, they had to camp
on the field, for they were getting well eastward.
They made a good many inquiries as to the location
of that indefinite "certain point," but got no information. At last, to a peculiarly urgent inquiry
of "How far eastward?" Governor Nye telegraphed
back:

"To the Atlantic Ocean, blast you!—and then
bridge it and go on!"

This brought back the dusty toilers, who sent in a
report and ceased from their labors. The Governor
was always comfortable about it; he said Mrs.
O'Flannigan would hold him for the Brigade's
board anyhow, and he intended to get what entertainment he could out of the boys; he said, with his
old-time pleasant twinkle, that he meant to survey
them into Utah and then telegraph Brigham to hang
them for trespass!

The surveyors brought back more tarantulas with
them, and so we had quite a menagerie arranged
along the shelves of the room. Some of these
spiders could straddle over a common saucer with
their hairy, muscular legs, and when their feelings
were hurt, or their dignity offended, they were the
wickedest-looking desperadoes the animal world can
furnish. If their glass prison-houses were touched
ever so lightly they were up and spoiling for a fight
in a minute. Starchy?—proud? Indeed, they
would take up a straw and pick their teeth like a
member of Congress. There was as usual a furious

"zephyr" blowing the first night of the Brigade's return, and about midnight the roof of an adjoining stable blew off, and a corner of it came crashing through the side of our ranch.   There was a simultaneous awakening, and a tumultuous muster of the Brigade in the dark, and a general tumbling and sprawling over each other in the narrow aisle between the bed-rows.   In the midst of the turmoil, Bob H—— sprung up out of a sound sleep, and knocked down a shelf with his head.   Instantly he shouted :

"Turn out, boys — the tarantulas is loose!"

No warning ever sounded so dreadful.   Nobody tried, any longer, to leave the room, lest he might step on a tarantula.   Every man groped for a trunk or a bed, and jumped on it.   Then followed the strangest silence — a silence of grisly suspense it was, too — waiting, expectancy, fear.   It was as dark as pitch, and one had to imagine the spectacle of those fourteen scant-clad men roosting gingerly on trunks and beds, for not a thing could be seen. Then came occasional little interruptions of the silence, and one could recognize a man and tell his locality by his voice, or locate any other sound a sufferer made by his gropings or changes of position.   The occasional voices were not given to much speaking — you simply heard a gentle ejaculation of "Ow!" followed by a solid thump, and you knew the gentleman had felt a hairy blanket or something touch his bare skin and had skipped from a bed to

12.

the floor.   Another silence.   Presently you would
hear a gasping voice say:

" Su-su-something's crawling up the back of my
neck !''

Every now and then you could hear a little sub-
dued scramble and a sorrowful " O Lord!" and then
you knew that somebody was getting away from
something he took for a tarantula, and not losing
any time about it, either.   Directly a voice in the
corner rang out wild and clear:

"I've got him!   I've got him!''   [Pause, and
probable change of circumstances.]   " No, he's got
me!   Oh, ain't they *never* going to fetch a lantern!''

The lantern came at that moment, in the hands of
Mrs. O'Flannigan, whose anxiety to know the
amount of damage done by the assaulting roof had
not prevented her waiting a judicious interval, after
getting out of bed and lighting up, to see if the wind
was done, now, up stairs, or had a larger contract.

The landscape presented when the lantern flashed
into the room was picturesque, and might have been
funny to some people, but was not to us.   Although
we were perched so strangely upon boxes, trunks
and beds, and so strangely attired, too, we were too
earnestly distressed and too genuinely miserable to
see any fun about it, and there was not the semblance of a smile anywhere visible.   I know I am
not capable of suffering more than I did during those
few minutes of suspense in the dark, surrounded by
those creeping, bloody-minded tarantulas.   I had

skipped from bed to bed and from box to box in a cold agony, and every time I touched anything that was fuzzy I fancied I felt the fangs. I had rather go to war than live that episode over again. Nobody was hurt. The man who thought a tarantula had " got him " was mistaken — only a crack in a box had caught his finger. Not one of those escaped tarantulas was ever seen again. There were ten or twelve of them. We took candles and hunted the place high and low for them, but with no success. Did we go back to bed then? We did nothing of the kind. Money could not have persuaded us to do it. We sat up the rest of the night playing cribbage and keeping a sharp lookout for the enemy.

CHAPTER XXII.

IT was the end of August, and the skies were cloudless and the weather superb. In two or three
weeks I had grown wonderfully fascinated with the
curious new country, and concluded to put off my
return to "the States" awhile. I had grown well
accustomed to wearing a damaged slouch hat, blue
woolen shirt, and pants crammed into boot-tops, and
gloried in the absence of coat, vest, and braces. I
felt rowdyish and "bully," (as the historian
Josephus phrases it, in his fine chapter upon the destruction of the Temple). It seemed to me that
nothing could be so fine and so romantic. I had become an officer of the government, but that was for
mere sublimity. The office was an unique sinecure.
I had nothing to do and no salary. I was private
secretary to his majesty the Secretary, and there was
not yet writing enough for two of us. So Johnny
K—— and I devoted our time to amusement. He
was the young son of an Ohio nabob and was out
there for recreation. He got it. We had heard a
world of talk about the marvelous beauty of Lake
Tahoe, and finally curiosity drove us thither to see

it. Three or four members of the Brigade had been there and located some timber lands on its shores and stored up a quantity of provisions in their camp. We strapped a couple of blankets on our shoulders and took an axe apiece and started — for we intended to take up a wood ranch or so ourselves and become wealthy. We were on foot. The reader will find it advantageous to go horseback. We were told that the distance was eleven miles. We tramped a long time on level ground, and then toiled laboriously up a mountain about a thousand miles high and looked over. No lake there. We descended on the other side, crossed the valley and toiled up another mountain three or four thousand miles high, apparently, and looked over again. No lake yet. We sat down tired and perspiring, and hired a couple of Chinamen to curse those people who had beguiled us. Thus refreshed, we presently resumed the march with renewed vigor and determination. We plodded on, two or three hours longer, and at last the Lake burst upon us — a noble sheet of blue water lifted six thousand three hundred feet above the level of the sea, and walled in by a rim of snow-clad mountain peaks that towered aloft full three thousand feet higher still! It was a vast oval, and one would have to use up eighty or a hundred good miles in traveling around it. As it lay there with the shadows of the mountains brilliantly photographed upon its still surface I thought it must surely be the fairest picture the whole earth affords.

We found the small skiff belonging to the Brigade boys, and without loss of time set out across a deep bend of the lake toward the landmarks that signified the locality of the camp. I got Johnny to row — not because I mind exertion myself, but because it makes me sick to ride backwards when I am at work. But I steered. A three-mile pull brought us to the camp just as the night fell, and we stepped ashore very tired and wolfishly hungry. In a "cache" among the rocks we found the provisions and the cooking utensils, and then, all fatigued as I was, I sat down on a boulder and superintended while Johnny gathered wood and cooked supper. Many a man who had gone through what I had, would have wanted to rest.

It was a delicious supper — hot bread, fried bacon, and black coffee. It was a delicious solitude we were in, too. Three miles away was a saw-mill and some workmen, but there were not fifteen other human beings throughout the wide circumference of the lake. As the darkness closed down and the stars came out and spangled the great mirror with jewels, we smoked meditatively in the solemn hush and forgot our troubles and our pains. In due time we spread our blankets in the warm sand between two large boulders and soon fell asleep, careless of the procession of ants that passed in through rents in our clothing and explored our persons. Nothing could disturb the sleep that fettered us, for it had been fairly earned, and if our consciences had any

sins on them they had to adjourn court for that
night, any way. The wind rose just as we were losing consciousness, and we were lulled to sleep by the
beating of the surf upon the shore.

It is always very cold on that lake shore in the
night, but we had plenty of blankets and were warm
enough. We never moved a muscle all night, but
waked at early dawn in the original positions, and
got up at once, thoroughly refreshed, free from sore-
ness, and brim full of friskiness. There is no end of
wholesome medicine in such an experience. That
morning we could have whipped ten such people as
we were the day before — sick ones at any rate.
But the world is slow, and people will go to " water
cures " and " movement cures " and to foreign lands
for health. Three months of camp life on Lake
Tahoe would restore an Egyptian mummy to his
pristine vigor, and give him an appetite like an alli-
gator. I do not mean the oldest and driest mum-
mies, of course, but the fresher ones. The air up
there in the clouds is very pure and fine, bracing
and delicious. And why shouldn't it be? — it is
the same the angels breathe. I think that hardly
any amount of fatigue can be gathered together
that a man cannot sleep off in one night on the sand
by its side. Not under a roof, but under the sky;
it seldom or never rains there in the summer time.
I know a man who went there to die. But he made
a failure of it. He was a skeleton when he came,
and could barely stand. He had no appetite, and

did nothing but read tracts and reflect on the future. Three months later he was sleeping out of doors regularly, eating all he could hold, three times a day, and chasing game over mountains three thousand feet high for recreation.   And he was a skeleton no longer, but weighed part of a ton.   This is no fancy sketch, but the truth.   His disease was consumption.   I confidently commend his experience to other skeletons.

I superintended again, and as soon as we had eaten breakfast we got in the boat and skirted along the lake shore about three miles and disembarked. We liked the appearance of the place, and so we claimed some three hundred acres of it and stuck our "notices" on a tree.   It was yellow pine timber land — a dense forest of trees a hundred feet high and from one to five feet through at the butt.   It was necessary to fence our property or we could not hold it.   That is to say, it was necessary to cut down trees here and there and make them fall in such a way as to form a sort of enclosure (with pretty wide gaps in it).   We cut down three trees apiece, and found it such heart-breaking work that we decided to "rest our case" on those; if they held the property, well and good; if they didn't, let the property spill out through the gaps and go; it was no use to work ourselves to death merely to save a few acres of land.   Next day we came back to build a house — for a house was also necessary, in order to hold the property.   We decided to build a sub-

stantial log-house and excite the envy of the Brigade
boys; but by the time we had cut and trimmed the
first log it seemed unnecessary to be so elaborate,
and so we concluded to build it of saplings.   However, two saplings, duly cut and trimmed, compelled
recognition of the fact that a still modester architec-
ture would satisfy the law, and so we concluded to
build a " brush " house.   We devoted the next day
to this work, but we did so much " sitting around "
and discussing, that by the middle of the afternoon
we had achieved only a half-way sort of affair which
one of us had to watch while the other cut brush,
lest if both turned our backs we might not be able
to find it again, it had such a strong family resemblance to the surrounding vegetation.   But we
were satisfied with it.

We were land owners now, duly seized and possessed, and within the protection of the law.   Therefore we decided to take up our residence on our own
domain and enjoy that large sense of independence
which only such an experience can bring.   Late the
next afternoon, after a good long rest, we sailed
away from the Brigade camp with all the provisions
and cooking utensils we could carry off — borrow is
the more accurate word — and just as the night was
falling we beached the boat at our own landing

CHAPTER XXIII.

IF there is any life that is happier than the life we led on our timber ranch for the next two or three weeks, it must be a sort of life which I have not read of in books or experienced in person. We did not see a human being but ourselves during the time, or hear any sounds but those that were made by the wind and the waves, the sighing of the pines, and now and then the far-off thunder of an avalanche. The forest about us was dense and cool, the sky above us was cloudless and brilliant with sunshine, the broad lake before us was glassy and clear, or rippled and breezy, or black and storm-tossed, according to Nature's mood; and its circling border of mountain domes, clothed with forests, scarred with landslides, cloven by canyons and valleys, and helmeted with glittering snow, fitly framed and finished the noble picture. The view was always fascinating, bewitching, entrancing. The eye was never tired of gazing, night or day, in calm or storm; it suffered but one grief, and that was that it could not look always, but must close sometimes in sleep.

We slept in the sand close to the water's edge, between two protecting boulders, which took care of the
stormy night-winds for us. We never took any pare-
goric to make us sleep. At the first break of dawn
we were always up and running foot-races to tone
down excess of physical vigor and exuberance of
spirits. That is, Johnny was — but I held his hat.
While smoking the pipe of peace after breakfast we
watched the sentinel peaks put on the glory of the
sun, and followed the conquering light as it swept
down among the shadows, and set the captive crags
and forests free. We watched the tinted pictures
grow and brighten upon the water till every little detail of forest, precipice, and pinnacle was wrought in
and finished, and the miracle of the enchanter complete. Then to "business."

That is, drifting around in the boat. We were on
the north shore. There, the rocks on the bottom
are sometimes gray, sometimes white. This gives
the marvelous transparency of the water a fuller advantage than it has elsewhere on the lake. We
usually pushed out a hundred yards or so from the
shore, and then lay down on the thwarts in the sun,
and let the boat drift by the hour whither it would.
We seldom talked. It interrupted the Sabbath stillness, and marred the dreams the luxurious rest and
indolence brought. The shore all along was in-
dented with deep, curved bays and coves, bordered
by narrow sand-beaches; and where the sand ended,
the steep mountain-sides rose right up aloft into
13

space — rose up like a vast wall a little out of the perpendicular, and thickly wooded with tall pines.

So singularly clear was the water, that where it was only twenty or thirty feet deep the bottom was so perfectly distinct that the boat seemed floating in the air! Yes, where it was even *eighty* feet deep. Every little pebble was distinct, every speckled trout, every hand's-breadth of sand. Often, as we lay on our faces, a granite boulder, as large as a village church, would start out of the bottom apparently, and seem climbing up rapidly to the surface, till presently it threatened to touch our faces, and we could not resist the impulse to seize an oar and avert the danger. But the boat would float on, and the boulder descend again, and then we could see that when we had been exactly above it, it must still have been twenty or thirty feet below the surface. Down through the transparency of these great depths, the water was not *merely* transparent, but dazzlingly, brilliantly so. All objects seen through it had a bright, strong vividness, not only of outline, but of every minute detail, which they would not have had when seen simply through the same depth of atmosphere. So empty and airy did all spaces seem below us, and so strong was the sense of floating high aloft in mid-nothingness, that we called these boat-excursions " balloon-voyages."

We fished a good deal, but we did not average one fish a week. We could see trout by the thousand winging about in the emptiness under us, or sleeping

in shoals on the bottom, but they would not bite —
they could see the line too plainly, perhaps. We
frequently selected the trout we wanted, and rested
the bait patiently and persistently on the end of his
nose at a depth of eighty feet, but he would only
shake it off with an annoyed manner, and shift his
position.

We bathed occasionally, but the water was rather
chilly, for all it looked so sunny. Sometimes we
rowed out to the " blue water," a mile or two from
shore. It was as dead blue as indigo there, because
of the immense depth. By official measurement,
the lake in its center is one thousand five hundred
and twenty-five feet deep !

Sometimes, on lazy afternoons, we lolled on the
sand in camp, and smoked pipes and read some old
well-worn novels. At night, by the camp-fire, we
played euchre and seven-up to strengthen the mind
— and played them with cards so greasy and defaced
that only a whole summer's acquaintance with them
could enable the student to tell the ace of clubs from
the jack of diamonds.

We never slept in our " house." It never occurred to us, for one thing; and besides, it was built
to hold the ground, and that was enough. We did
not wish to strain it.

By and by our provisions began to run short,
and we went back to the old camp and laid in a
new supply. We were gone all day, and reached
home again about nightfall, pretty tired and hungry.

While Johnny was carrying the main bulk of the provisions up to our " house " for future use, I took the loaf of bread, some slices of bacon, and the coffee-pot, ashore, set them down by a tree, lit a fire, and went back to the boat to get the frying-pan. While I was at this, I heard a shout from Johnny, and looking up I saw that my fire was galloping all over the premises!

Johnny was on the other side of it. He had to run through the flames to get to the lake shore, and then we stood helpless and watched the devastation.

The ground was deeply carpeted with dry pine-needles, and the fire touched them off as if they were gunpowder. It was wonderful to see with what fierce speed the tall sheet of flame traveled! My coffee-pot was gone, and everything with it. In a minute and a half the fire seized upon a dense growth of dry manzanita chapparal six or eight feet high, and then the roaring and popping and crackling was something terrific. We were driven to the boat by the intense heat, and there we remained, spell-bound.

Within half an hour all before us was a tossing, blinding tempest of flame! It went surging up adjacent ridges — surmounted them and disappeared in the canyons beyond — burst into view upon higher and farther ridges, presently — shed a grander illumination abroad, and dove again — flamed out again, directly, higher and still higher up the mountain-side — threw out skirmishing parties of fire here and there, and sent them trailing their crimson spirals away among remote ramparts and ribs and gorges, till as far as the eye could reach the lofty mountain-fronts were webbed as it were with a tangled network of red lava streams. Away across the water the crags and domes were lit with a ruddy glare, and the firmament above was a reflected hell!

Every feature of the spectacle was repeated in the glowing mirror of the lake! Both pictures were sublime, both were beautiful; but that in the lake had a bewildering richness about it that enchanted the eye and held it with the stronger fascination.

We sat absorbed and motionless through four long hours. We never thought of supper, and never felt fatigue. But at eleven o'clock the conflagration had traveled beyond our range of vision, and then darkness stole down upon the landscape again.

Hunger asserted itself now, but there was nothing to eat. The provisions were all cooked, no doubt, but we did not go to see. We were homeless wanderers again, without any property. Our fence was gone, our house burned down; no insurance. Our pine forest was well scorched, the dead trees all burned up, and our broad acres of manzanita swept away. Our blankets were on our usual sand-bed, however, and so we lay down and went to sleep. The next morning we started back to the old camp, but while out a long way from shore, so great a storm came up that we dared not try to land. So I bailed out the seas we shipped, and Johnny pulled heavily through the billows till we had reached a point three or four miles beyond the camp. The storm was increasing, and it became evident that it was better to take the hazard of beaching the boat than go down in a hundred fathoms of water; so we ran in, with tall white-caps following, and I sat down in the stern-sheets and pointed her head-on to the shore. The instant the bow struck, a wave came over the stern that washed crew and cargo ashore, and saved a deal of trouble. We shivered in the lee of a boulder all the rest of the day, and froze all the night through. In the morning the tempest had gone down, and we paddled down to the camp without any unnecessary delay. We were so starved that we ate up the rest of the Brigade's provisions, and then set out to Carson to tell them about it and ask their forgiveness. It was accorded, upon payment of damages.

We made many trips to the lake after that, and had many a hair-breadth escape and blood-curdling adventure which will never be recorded of any history.

CHAPTER XXIV.

I RESOLVED to have a horse to ride. I had never seen such wild, free, magnificent horsemanship outside of a circus as these picturesquely-clad Mexicans, Californians, and Mexicanized Americans displayed in Carson streets every day. How they rode! Leaning just gently forward out of the perpendicular, easy and nonchalant, with broad slouch-hat brim blown square up in front, and long *riata* swinging above the head, they swept through the town like the wind! The next minute they were only a sailing puff of dust on the far desert. If they trotted, they sat up gallantly and gracefully, and seemed part of the horse; did not go jiggering up and down after the silly Miss-Nancy fashion of the riding-schools. I had quickly learned to tell a horse from a cow, and was full of anxiety to learn more. I was resolved to buy a horse.

While the thought was rankling in my mind, the auctioneer came scurrying through the plaza on a black beast that had as many humps and corners on him as a dromedary, and was necessarily uncomely; but he was "going, going, at twenty-two! — horse,

13.*   (193)

saddle and bridle at twenty-two dollars, gentlemen!'' and I could hardly resist.

A man whom I did not know (he turned out to
be the auctioneer's brother) noticed the wistful look in
my eye, and observed that that was a very remarkable
horse to be going at such a price; and added that
the saddle alone was worth the money. It was a
Spanish saddle, with ponderous *tapidaros*, and
furnished with the ungainly sole-leather covering
with the unspellable name. I said I had half a
notion to bid. Then this keen-eyed person appeared
to me to be '' taking my measure''; but I dismissed
the suspicion when he spoke, for his manner was
full of guileless candor and truthfulness. Said he:

'' I know that horse — know him well. You are a
stranger, I take it, and so you might think he was
an American horse, maybe, but I assure you he is
not. He is nothing of the kind; but — excuse my
speaking in a low voice, other people being near —
he is, without the shadow of a doubt, a Genuine
Mexican Plug!''

I did not know what a Genuine Mexican Plug was,
but there was something about this man's way of
saying it, that made me swear inwardly that I would
own a Genuine Mexican Plug, or die.

'' Has he any other — er — advantages?'' I in-
quired, suppressing what eagerness I could.

He hooked his forefinger in the pocket of my
army-shirt, led me to one side, and breathed in my
ear impressively these words:

"He can out-buck anything in America!"

"Going, going, going — at *twent–ty*-four dollars and a half, gen —" "Twenty-seven!" I shouted, in a frenzy.

"And sold!" said the auctioneer, and passed over the Genuine Mexican Plug to me.

I could scarcely contain my exultation. I paid the money, and put the animal in a neighboring livery-stable to dine and rest himself.

In the afternoon I brought the creature into the plaza, and certain citizens held him by the head, and others by the tail, while I mounted him. As soon as they let go, he placed all his feet in a bunch together, lowered his back, and then suddenly arched it upward, and shot me straight into the air a matter of three or four feet! I came as straight down again, lit in the saddle, went instantly up again, came down almost on the high pommel, shot up again, and came down on the horse's neck — all in the space of three or four seconds. Then he rose and stood almost straight up on his hind feet, and I, clasping his lean neck desperately, slid back into the saddle, and held on. He came down, and immediately hoisted his heels into the air, delivering a vicious kick at the sky, and stood on his fore feet. And then down he came once more, and began the original exercise of shooting me straight up again.

The third time I went up I heard a stranger say: "Oh, *don't* he buck, though!"

While I was up, somebody struck the horse a

M*

sounding thwack with a leathern strap, and when I arrived again the Genuine Mexican Plug was not there. A Californian youth chased him up and caught him, and asked if he might have a ride. I granted him that luxury. He mounted the Genuine, got lifted into the air once, but sent his spurs home as he descended, and the horse darted away like a telegram. He soared over three fences like a bird, and disappeared down the road toward the Washoe Valley.

I sat down on a stone with a sigh, and by a natural impulse one of my hands sought my forehead, and the other the base of my stomach. I believe I never appreciated, till then, the poverty of the human machinery — for I still needed a hand or two to place elsewhere. Pen cannot describe how I was jolted up. Imagination cannot conceive how disjointed I was — how internally, externally, and universally I was unsettled, mixed up, and ruptured. There was a sympathetic crowd around me, though.

One elderly-looking comforter said:

" Stranger, you've been taken in. Everybody in this camp knows that horse. Any child, any Injun, could have told you that he'd buck; he is the very worst devil to buck on the continent of America. You hear *me*. I'm Curry. *Old* Curry. Old *Abe* Curry. And moreover, he is a simon-pure, out-and-out, genuine d—d Mexican plug, and an uncommon mean one at that, too. Why, you turnip, if you had laid low and kept dark, there's chances

to buy an *American* horse for mighty little more
than you paid for that bloody old foreign relic."

I gave no sign; but I made up my mind that if the
auctioneer's brother's funeral took place while I
was in the Territory I would postpone all other
recreations and attend it.

After a gallop of sixteen miles the Californian
youth and the Genuine Mexican Plug came tearing
into town again, shedding foam-flakes like the spume-
spray that drives before a typhoon, and, with one
final skip over a wheelbarrow and a Chinaman, cast
anchor in front of the "ranch."

Such panting and blowing! Such spreading and
contracting of the red equine nostrils, and glaring
of the wild equine eye! But was the imperial beast
subjugated? Indeed, he was not. His lordship the
Speaker of the House thought he was, and mounted
him to go down to the Capitol; but the first dash the
creature made was over a pile of telegraph poles
half as high as a church; and his time to the Capitol — one mile and three-quarters — remains unbeaten to this day. But then he took an advantage
— he left out the mile, and only did the three-
quarters. That is to say, he made a straight cut
across lots, preferring fences and ditches to a
crooked road; and when the Speaker got to the
Capitol he said he had been in the air so much he
felt as if he had made the trip on a comet.

In the evening the Speaker came home afoot for
exercise, and got the Genuine towed back behind

a quartz wagon. The next day I loaned the animal to the Clerk of the House to go down to the Dana silver mine, six miles, and *he* walked back for exercise, and got the horse towed. Everybody I loaned him to always walked back; they never could get enough exercise any other way. Still, I continued to loan him to anybody who was willing to borrow him, my idea being to get him crippled, and throw him on the borrower's hands, or killed, and make the borrower pay for him. But somehow nothing ever happened to him. He took chances that no other horse ever took and survived, but he always came out safe. It was his daily habit to try experiments that had always before been considered impossible, but he always got through. Sometimes he miscalculated a little, and did not get his rider through intact, but *he* always got through himself. Of course I had tried to sell him; but that was a stretch of simplicity which met with little sympathy. The auctioneer stormed up and down the streets on him for four days, dispersing the populace, interrupting business, and destroying children, and never got a bid — at least never any but the eighteen-dollar one he hired a notoriously substanceless bummer to make. The people only smiled pleasantly, and restrained their desire to buy, if they had any. Then the auctioneer brought in his bill, and I withdrew the horse from the market. We tried to trade him off at private vendue next, offering him at a sacrifice for second-hand tombstones, old iron, temperance tracts — any kind of property. But holders were stiff, and we retired from the market again. I never tried to ride the horse any more. Walking was good enough exercise for a man like me, that had nothing the matter with him except ruptures, internal injuries, and such things. Finally I tried to *give* him away. But it was a failure. Parties said earthquakes were handy enough on the Pacific coast — they did not wish to own one. As a last resort I offered him to the Governor for the use of the "Brigade." His face lit up eagerly at first, but toned down again, and he said the thing would be too palpable.

Just then the livery stable man brought in his bill for six weeks' keeping — stall-room for the horse, fifteen dollars; hay for the horse, two hundred and fifty! The Genuine Mexican Plug had eaten a ton of the article, and the man said he would have eaten a hundred if he had let him.

I will remark here, in all seriousness, that the regular price of hay during that year and a part of the next was really two hundred and fifty dollars a ton. During a part of the previous year it had sold at five hundred a ton, in gold, and during the winter before that there was such scarcity of the article that in several instances small quantities had brought eight hundred dollars a ton in coin! The consequence might be guessed without my telling it: people turned their stock loose to starve, and before the spring arrived Carson and Eagle Valleys were almost literally carpeted with their carcasses! Any old settler there will verify these statements.

I managed to pay the livery bill, and that same day I gave the Genuine Mexican Plug to a passing Arkansas emigrant whom fortune delivered into my hand. If this ever meets his eye, he will doubtless remember the donation.

Now whoever has had the luck to ride a real Mexican plug will recognize the animal depicted in this chapter, and hardly consider him exaggerated — but the uninitiated will feel justified in regarding his portrait as a fancy sketch, perhaps.

CHAPTER XXV.

ORIGINALLY, Nevada was a part of Utah and was called Carson County; and a pretty large county it was, too. Certain of its valleys produced no end of hay, and this attracted small colonies of Mormon stock-raisers and farmers to them. A few orthodox Americans straggled in from California, but no love was lost between the two classes of colonists. There was little or no friendly intercourse; each party staid to itself. The Mormons were largely in the majority, and had the additional advantage of being peculiarly under the protection of the Mormon government of the Territory. Therefore they could afford to be distant, and even peremptory toward their neighbors. One of the traditions of Carson Valley illustrates the condition of things that prevailed at the time I speak of. The hired girl of one of the American families was Irish, and a Catholic; yet it was noted with surprise that she was the only person outside of the Mormon ring who could get favors from the Mormons. She asked kindnesses of them often, and always got them. It was a mystery to everybody. But one

day as she was passing out at the door, a large bowie
knife dropped from under her apron, and when her
mistress asked for an explanation she observed that
she was going out to "borry a wash-tub from the
Mormons!"

In 1858 silver lodes were discovered in "Carson
County," and then the aspect of things changed.
Californians began to flock in, and the American
element was soon in the majority. Allegiance to Brigham Young and Utah was renounced, and a temporary Territorial government for "Washoe" was
instituted by the citizens. Governor Roop was the
first and only chief magistrate of it. In due course
of time Congress passed a bill to organize "Nevada
Territory," and President Lincoln sent out Governor
Nye to supplant Roop.

At this time the population of the Territory was
about twelve or fifteen thousand, and rapidly increasing. Silver mines were being vigorously developed and silver mills erected. Business of all
kinds was active and prosperous and growing more
so day by day.

The people were glad to have a legitimately
constituted government, but did not particularly
enjoy having strangers from distant States put in
authority over them — a sentiment that was natural
enough. They thought the officials should have
been chosen from among themselves — from among
prominent citizens who had earned a right to such
promotion, and who would be in sympathy with the

populace and likewise thoroughly acquainted with
the needs of the Territory.   They were right in viewing the matter thus, without doubt.   The new
officers were "emigrants," and that was no title to
anybody's affection or admiration either.

The new government was received with considerable coolness.   It was not only a foreign intruder,
but a poor one.   It was not even worth plucking
— except by the smallest of small fry office-seek-
ers and such.   Everybody knew that Congress had
appropriated only twenty thousand dollars a year in
greenbacks for its support — about money enough
to run a quartz mill a month.   And everybody
knew, also, that the first year's money was still in
Washington, and that the getting hold of it would
be a tedious and difficult process.   Carson City was
too wary and too wise to open up a credit account
with the imported bantling with anything like in-
decent haste.

There is something solemnly funny about the
struggles of a new-born Territorial government to
get a start in this world.   Ours had a trying time of
it.   The Organic Act and the "instructions" from
the State Department commanded that a legislature
should be elected at such-and-such a time, and its
sittings inaugurated at such-and-such a date.   It
was easy to get legislators, even at three dollars a
day, although board was four dollars and fifty
cents, for distinction has its charm in Nevada as well
as elsewhere, and there were plenty of patriotic souls
14

out of employment; but to get a legislative hall for
them to meet in was another matter altogether.
Carson blandly declined to give a room rent-free, or
let one to the government on credit.

But when Curry heard of the difficulty, he came
forward, solitary and alone, and shouldered the Ship
of State over the bar and got her afloat again.   I
refer to " Curry — *Old* Curry — Old *Abe* Curry."
But for him the legislature would have been obliged
to sit in the desert.   He offered his large stone
building just outside the capital limits, rent-free, and
it was gladly accepted.   Then he built a horse-rail-
road from town to the capitol, and carried the legislators gratis.   He also furnished pine benches and
chairs for the legislature, and covered the floors
with clean saw-dust by way of carpet and spittoon
combined.   But for Curry the government would
have died in its tender infancy.   A canvas partition
to separate the Senate from the House of Representatives was put up by the Secretary, at a cost of
three dollars and forty cents, but the United States
declined to pay for it.   Upon being reminded that
the " instructions " permitted the payment of a
liberal rent for a legislative hall, and that that money
was saved to the country by Mr. Curry's generosity,
the United States said that did not alter the matter,
and the three dollars and forty cents would be sub-
tracted from the Secretary's eighteen hundred dollar salary — and it *was!*

The matter of printing was from the beginning an

interesting feature of the new government's difficulties. The Secretary was sworn to obey his volume of written "instructions," and these commanded him to do two certain things without fail, viz.:

1. Get the House and Senate journals printed; and,

2. For this work, pay one dollar and fifty cents per "thousand" for composition, and one dollar and fifty cents per "token" for press-work, in greenbacks.

It was easy to swear to do these two things, but it was entirely impossible to do more than one of them. When greenbacks had gone down to forty cents on the dollar, the prices regularly charged everybody by printing establishments were one dollar and fifty cents per "thousand" and one dollar and fifty cents per "token," in *gold*. The "instructions" commanded that the Secretary regard a paper dollar issued by the government as equal to any other dollar issued by the government. Hence the printing of the journals was discontinued. Then the United States sternly rebuked the Secretary for disregarding the "instructions," and warned him to correct his ways. Wherefore he got some printing done, forwarded the bill to Washington with full exhibits of the high prices of things in the Territory, and called attention to a printed market report wherein it would be observed that even hay was two hundred and fifty dollars a ton. The United States responded by subtracting the printing-bill from the

Secretary's suffering salary — and moreover remarked with dense gravity that he would find nothing
in his "instructions" requiring him to purchase
hay !

Nothing in this world is palled in such impene-
trable obscurity as a U. S. Treasury Comptroller's
understanding. The very fires of the hereafter could
get up nothing more than a fitful glimmer in it.
In the days I speak of he never could be made to
comprehend why it was that twenty thousand dollars
would not go as far in Nevada, where all commodi-
ties ranged at an enormous figure, as it would in the
other Territories, where exceeding cheapness was
the rule.   He was an officer who looked out for the
little expenses all the time.   The Secretary of the
Territory kept his office in his bedroom, as I before
remarked; and he charged the United States no
rent, although his "instructions" provided for that
item, and he could have justly taken advantage of it
(a thing which I would have done with more than
lightning promptness if I had been Secretary myself).   But the United States never applauded this
devotion.   Indeed,   I think   my   country   was
ashamed to have so improvident a person in its
employ.

Those "instructions" (we used to read a chapter
from them every morning, as intellectual gymnas-
tics, and a couple of chapters in Sunday-school every
Sabbath, for they treated of all subjects under the
sun and had much valuable religious matter in them

along with the other statistics) those "instructions" commanded that pen-knives, envelopes, pens, and writing-paper be furnished the members of the legislature. So the Secretary made the purchase and the distribution. The knives cost three dollars apiece. There was one too many, and the Secretary gave it to the Clerk of the House of Representatives. The United States said the Clerk of the House was not a "member" of the legislature, and took that three dollars out of the Secretary's salary, as usual.

White men charged three or four dollars a "load" for sawing up stove-wood. The Secretary was sagacious enough to know that the United States would never pay any such price as that; so he got an Indian to saw up a load of office wood at one dollar and a half. He made out the usual voucher, but signed no name to it — simply appended a note explaining that an Indian had done the work, and had done it in a very capable and satisfactory way, but could not sign the voucher owing to lack of ability in the necessary direction. The Secretary had to pay that dollar and a half. He thought the United States would admire both his economy and his honesty in getting the work done at half price and not putting a pretended Indian's signature to the voucher, but the United States did not see it in that light. The United States was too much accustomed to employing dollar-and-a-half thieves in all manner of official capacities to regard his explanation of the voucher as having any foundation in fact.

But the next time the Indian sawed wood for us I taught him to make a cross at the bottom of the voucher — it looked like a cross that had been drunk a year — and then I "witnessed" it and it went through all right. The United States never said a word. I was sorry I had not made the voucher for a thousand loads of wood instead of one. The government of my country snubs honest simplicity, but fondles artistic villainy, and I think I might have developed into a very capable pickpocket if I had remained in the public service a year or two.

That was a fine collection of sovereigns, that first Nevada legislature. They levied taxes to the amount of thirty or forty thousand dollars and ordered expenditures to the extent of about a million. Yet they had their little periodical explosions of economy like all other bodies of the kind. A member proposed to save three dollars a day to the nation by dispensing with the Chaplain. And yet that short-sighted man needed the Chaplain more than any other member, perhaps, for he generally sat with his feet on his desk, eating raw turnips, during the morning prayer.

The legislature sat sixty days, and passed private toll-road franchises all the time. When they adjourned it was estimated that every citizen owned about three franchises, and it was believed that unless Congress gave the Territory another degree of longitude there would not be room enough to accommodate the toll-roads. The ends of them were hanging over the boundary line everywhere like a fringe.

The fact is, the freighting business had grown to such important proportions that there was nearly as much excitement over suddenly acquired toll-road fortunes as over the wonderful silver mines.

CHAPTER XXVI

BY and by I was smitten with the silver fever. "Prospecting parties" were leaving for the mountains every day, and discovering and taking possession of rich silver-bearing lodes and ledges of quartz. Plainly this was the road to fortune. The great "Gould and Curry" mine was held at three or four hundred dollars a foot when we arrived; but in two months it had sprung up to eight hundred. The "Ophir" had been worth only a mere trifle, a year gone by, and now it was selling at nearly *four thousand dollars a foot!* Not a mine could be named that had not experienced an astonishing advance in value within a short time. Everybody was talking about these marvels. Go where you would, you heard nothing else, from morning till far into the night. Tom So-and-So had sold out of the "Amanda Smith" for $40,000 — hadn't a cent when he "took up" the ledge six months ago. John Jones had sold half his interest in the "Bald Eagle and Mary Ann" for $65,000, gold coin, and gone to the States for his family. The widow Brewster had "struck it rich" in the "Golden

Fleece " and sold ten feet for $18,000 — hadn't
money enough to buy a crape bonnet when Sing-
Sing Tommy killed her husband at Baldy Johnson's
wake last spring. The " Last Chance " had found
a " clay casing " and knew they were " right on the
ledge "—consequence, "feet" that went begging
yesterday were worth a brick house apiece to-day,
and seedy owners who could not get trusted for a
drink at any bar in the country yesterday were
roaring drunk on champagne to-day and had hosts
of warm personal friends in a town where they had
forgotten how to bow or shake hands from long-
continued want of practice. Johnny Morgan, a
common loafer, had gone to sleep in the gutter and
waked up worth a hundred thousand dollars, in consequence of the decision in the " Lady Franklin and
Rough and Ready " lawsuit. And so on — day in
and day out the talk pelted our ears and the excitement waxed hotter and hotter around us.

I would have been more or less than human if I
had not gone mad like the rest. Cart-loads of solid
silver bricks, as large as pigs of lead, were arriving
from the mills every day, and such sights as that
gave substance to the wild talk about me. I succumbed and grew as frenzied as the craziest.

.Every few days news would come of the discovery
of a bran-new mining region; immediately the
papers would teem with accounts of its richness,
and away the surplus population would scamper to
take possession. By the time I was fairly inocu-

N*

lated with the disease, "Esmeralda" had just had
a run and "Humboldt" was beginning to shriek
for attention. "Humboldt! Humboldt!" was the
new cry, and straightway Humboldt, the newest of
the new, the richest of the rich, the most marvelous
of the marvelous discoveries in silver-land, was occupying two columns of the public prints to "Esmeralda's" one. I was just on the point of starting to
Esmeralda, but turned with the tide and got ready
for Humboldt. That the reader may see what
moved me, and what would as surely have moved
him had he been there, I insert here one of the
newspaper letters of the day. It and several other
letters from the same calm hand were the main
means of converting me. I shall not garble the
extract, but put it in just as it appeared in the *Daily
Territorial Enterprise:*

But what about our mines ? I shall be candid with you. I shall express an honest opinion, based upon a thorough examination. Humboldt county is the richest mineral region upon God's footstool. Each
mountain range is gorged with the precious ores. Humboldt is the
true Golconda.

The other day an assay of mere *croppings* yielded exceeding *four
thousand dollars to the ton.* A week or two ago an assay of just such
surface developments made returns of *seven thousand* dollars to the ton.
Our mountains are full of rambling prospectors. Each day and almost
every hour reveals new and more startling evidences of the profuse and
intensified wealth of our favored county. The metal is not silver alone.
There are distinct ledges of auriferous ore. A late discovery plainly
evinces cinnabar. The coarser metals are in gross abundance. Lately
evidences of bituminous coal have been detected. My theory has ever
been that coal is a ligneous formation. I told Col. Whitman, in times
past, that the neighborhood of Dayton (Nevada) betrayed no present or

previous manifestations of a ligneous foundation, and that hence I had no confidence in his lauded coal mines. I repeated the same doctrine to the exultant coal discoverers of Humboldt. I talked with my friend Captain Burch on the subject. My pyrhanism vanished upon his statement that in the very region referred to he had seen petrified trees of the length of two hundred feet. Then is the fact established that huge forests once cast their grim shadows over this remote section. I am firm in the coal faith. Have no fears of the mineral resources of Humboldt county. They are immense — incalculable.

Let me state one or two things which will help the reader to better comprehend certain items in the above. At this time, our near neighbor, Gold Hill, was the most successful silver - mining locality in Nevada. It was from there that more than half the daily shipments of silver bricks came. "Very rich" (and scarce) Gold Hill ore yielded from $100 to $400 to the ton; but the usual yield was only $20 to $40 per ton — that is to say, each hundred pounds of ore yielded from one dollar to two dollars. But the reader will perceive by the above extract, that in Humboldt from one-fourth to nearly half the mass was silver! That is to say, every one hundred pounds of the ore had from *two hundred* dollars up to about *three hundred and fifty* in it. Some days later this same correspondent wrote:

I have spoken of the vast and almost fabulous wealth of this region —it is incredible. The intestines of our mountains are gorged with precious ore to plethora. I have said that nature has so shaped our mountains as to furnish most excellent facilities for the working of our mines. I have also told you that the country about here is pregnant with the finest mill sites in the world. But what is the mining history of Humboldt? The Sheba mine is in the hands of energetic San Francisco capitalists. It would seem that the ore is combined with metals that render it difficult of reduction with our imperfect mountain machinery. The proprietors have combined the capital and labor hinted at in my exordium. They are toiling and probing. Their tunnel has reached the length of one hundred feet. From primal assays alone, coupled with the development of the mine and public confidence in the continuance of effort, the stock had reared itself to eight hundred dollars market value. I do not know that one ton of the ore has been converted into current metal. I do know that there are many lodes in this section that surpass the Sheba in primal assay value. Listen a moment to the calculations of the Sheba operators. They purpose transporting the ore concentrated to Europe. The conveyance from Star City (its locality) to Virginia City will cost seventy dollars per ton ; from Virginia to San Francisco, forty dollars per ton ; from thence to Liverpool, its destination, ten dollars per ton. Their idea is that its conglomerate metals will reimburse them their cost of original extraction, the price of transportation, and the expense of reduction, and that then a ton of the raw ore will net them twelve hundred dollars. The estimate may be extravagant. Cur it in twain, and the product is enormous, far transcending any previous developments of our racy Territory.

A very common calculation is that many of our mines will yield five hundred dollars to the ton. Such fecundity throws the Gould & Curry, the Ophir and the Mexican, of your neighborhood, in the darkest shadow. I have given you the estimate of the value of a single developed mine. Its richness is indexed by its market valuation. The people of Humboldt county are *feet* crazy. As I write, our towns are near deserted. They look as languid as a consumptive girl. What has become of our sinewy and athletic fellow-citizens ? They are coursing through ravines and over mountain tops. Their tracks are visible in every direction. Occasionally a horseman will dash among us. His steed betrays hard usage. He alights before his a/lobe dwelling, hastily exchanges courtesies with his townsmen, hurries to an assay office and from thence to the District Recorder's. In the morning, having renewed his provisional supplies, he is off again on his wild and unbeaten route. Why, the fellow numbers already his feet by the thousands. He is the horse-leech. He has the craving stomach of the shark or anaconda. He would conquer metallic worlds.

This was enough. The instant we had finished reading the above article, four of us decided to go

to Humboldt. We commenced getting ready at
once. And we also commenced upbraiding ourselves for not deciding sooner — for we were in
terror lest all the rich mines would be found and
secured before we got there, and we might have to
put up with ledges that would not yield more than
two or three hundred dollars a ton, maybe. An
hour before, I would have felt opulent if I had
owned ten feet in a Gold Hill mine whose ore produced twenty-five dollars to the ton; now I was
already annoyed at the prospect of having to put up
with mines the poorest of which would be a marvel
in Gold Hill.

CHAPTER XXVII.

HURRY, was the word! We wasted no time. Our party consisted of four persons — a black-smith sixty years of age, two young lawyers, and myself. We bought a wagon and two miserable old horses. We put eighteen hundred pounds of provisions and mining tools in the wagon and drove out of Carson on a chilly December afternoon. The horses were so weak and old that we soon found that it would be better if one or two of us got out and walked. It was an improvement. Next, we found that it would be better if a third man got out. That was an improvement also. It was at this time that I volunteered to drive, although I had never driven a harnessed horse before, and many a man in such a position would have felt fairly ex-cused from such a responsibility. But in a little while it was found that it would be a fine thing if the driver got out and walked also. It was at this time that I resigned the position of driver, and never resumed it again. Within the hour, we found that it would not only be better, but was absolutely necessary, that we four, taking turns, two at a time, should put our hands against the end of the wagon and push it through the sand, leaving the feeble horses little to do but keep out of the way and hold up the tongue. Perhaps it is well for one to know his fate at first, and get reconciled to it. We had learned ours in one afternoon. It was plain that we had to walk through the sand and shove that wagon and those horses two hundred miles. So we accepted the situation, and from that time forth we never rode. More than that, we stood regular and nearly constant watches pushing up behind.

We made seven miles, and camped in the desert. Young Claggett (now member of Congress from Montana) unharnessed and fed and watered the horses; Oliphant and I cut sage-brush, built the fire and brought water to cook with; and old Mr. Ballou, the blacksmith, did the cooking. This division of labor, and this appointment, was adhered to throughout the journey. We had no tent, and so we slept under our blankets in the open plain. We were so tired that we slept soundly.

We were fifteen days making the trip — two hundred miles; thirteen, rather, for we lay by a couple of days, in one place, to let the horses rest. We could really have accomplished the journey in ten days if we had towed the horses behind the wagon, but we did not think of that until it was too late, and so went on shoving the horses and the wagon too when we might have saved half the labor. Parties who met us, occasionally, advised us to put

the horses *in* the wagon, but Mr. Ballou, through
whose iron-clad earnestness no sarcasm could pierce,
said that that would not do, because the provisions
were exposed and would suffer, the horses being
"bituminous from long deprivation." The reader
will excuse me from translating. What Mr. Ballou
customarily meant, when he used a long word, was
a secret between himself and his Maker. He was
one of the best and kindest-hearted men that ever
graced a humble sphere of life. He was gentleness
and simplicity itself — and unselfishness, too.
Although he was more than twice as old as the
eldest of us, he never gave himself any airs,
privileges, or exemptions on that account. He did
a *young* man's share of the work; and did his share
of conversing and entertaining from the general
standpoint of *any* age — not from the arrogant,
overawing summit-height of sixty years. His one
striking peculiarity was his Partingtonian fashion of
loving and using big words *for their own sakes*, and
independent of any bearing they might have upon
the thought he was purposing to convey. He
always let his ponderous syllables fall with an easy
unconsciousness that left them wholly without
offensiveness. In truth, his air was so natural and
so simple that one was always catching himself ac-
cepting his stately sentences as meaning something,
when they really meant nothing in the world. If a
word was long and grand and resonant, that was
sufficient to win the old man's love, and he would

drop that word into the most out-of-the-way place in a sentence or a subject, and be as pleased with it as if it were perfectly luminous with meaning.

We four always spread our common stock of blankets together on the frozen ground, and slept side by side; and finding that our foolish, long-legged hound pup had a deal of animal heat in him, Oliphant got to admitting him to the bed, between himself and Mr. Ballou, hugging the dog's warm back to his breast and finding great comfort in it. But in the night the pup would get stretchy and brace his feet against the old man's back and shove, grunting complacently the while; and now and then, being warm and snug, grateful and happy, he would paw the old man's back simply in excess of comfort; and at yet other times he would dream of the chase and in his sleep tug at the old man's back hair and bark in his ear. The old gentleman complained mildly about these familiarities, at last, and when he got through with his statement he said that such a dog as that was not a proper animal to admit to bed with tired men, because he was " so meretricious in his movements and so organic in his emotions.'' We turned the dog out.

It was a hard, wearing, toilsome journey, but it had its bright side; for after each day was done and our wolfish hunger appeased with a hot supper of fried bacon, bread, molasses, and black coffee, the pipe-smoking, song-singing, and yarn-spinning around the evening camp-fire in the still solitudes

15

of the desert was a happy, care-free sort of recreation that seemed the very summit and culmination
of earthly luxury. It is a kind of life that has a
potent charm for all men, whether city or country-
bred. We are descended from desert-lounging
Arabs, and countless ages of growth toward perfect
civilization have failed to root out of us the nomadic
instinct. We all confess to a gratified thrill at the
thought of "camping out."

Once we made twenty-five miles in a day, and
once we made forty miles (through the Great
American Desert), and ten miles beyond — fifty in
all — in twenty-three hours, without halting to eat,
drink, or rest. To stretch out and go to sleep, even
on stony and frozen ground, after pushing a wagon
and two horses fifty miles, is a delight so supreme
that for the moment it almost seems cheap at the
price.

We camped two days in the neighborhood of the
"Sink of the Humboldt." We tried to use the
strong alkaline water of the Sink, but it would not
answer. It was like drinking lye, and not weak lye,
either. It left a taste in the mouth, bitter and every
way execrable, and a burning in the stomach that
was very uncomfortable. We put molasses in it,
but that helped it very little; we added a pickle, yet
the alkali was the prominent taste, and so it was
unfit for drinking. The coffee we made of this
water was the meanest compound man has yet in-
vented. It was really viler to the taste than the

unameliorated water itself. Mr. Ballou, being the architect and builder of the beverage, felt constrained to endorse and uphold it, and so drank half a cup, by little sips, making shift to praise it faintly the while, but finally threw out the remainder, and said frankly it was "too technical for *him*."

But presently we found a spring of fresh water, convenient, and then, with nothing to mar our enjoyment, and no stragglers to interrupt it, we entered into our rest.

CHAPTER XXVIII.

AFTER leaving the Sink, we traveled along the Humboldt river a little way. People accustomed to the monster mile-wide Mississippi, grow accustomed to associating the term "river" with a high degree of watery grandeur. Consequently, such people feel rather disappointed when they stand on the shores of the Humboldt or the Carson and find that a "river" in Nevada is a sickly rivulet which is just the counterpart of the Erie canal in all respects save that the canal is twice as long and four times as deep. One of the pleasantest and most invigorating exercises one can contrive is to run and jump across the Humboldt river till he is overheated, and then drink it dry.

On the fifteenth day we completed our march of two hundred miles and entered Unionville, Humboldt County, in the midst of a driving snow-storm. Unionville consisted of eleven cabins and a liberty-pole. Six of the cabins were strung along one side of a deep canyon, and the other five faced them. The rest of the landscape was made up of bleak mountain walls that rose so high into the sky from both sides of the canyon that the village was left, as it were, far down in the bottom of a crevice. It was always daylight on the mountain tops a long time before the darkness lifted and revealed Unionville.

We built a small, rude cabin in the side of the crevice and roofed it with canvas, leaving a corner open to serve as a chimney, through which the cattle used to tumble occasionally, at night, and mash our furniture and interrupt our sleep. It was very cold weather and fuel was scarce. Indians brought brush and bushes several miles on their backs; and when we could catch a laden Indian it was well—and when we could not (which was the rule, not the exception), we shivered and bore it.

I confess, without shame, that I expected to find masses of silver lying all about the ground. I expected to see it glittering in the sun on the mountain summits. I said nothing about this, for some instinct told me that I might possibly have an exaggerated idea about it, and so if I betrayed my thought I might bring derision upon myself. Yet I was as perfectly satisfied in my own mind as I could be of anything, that I was going to gather up, in a day or two, or at furthest a week or two, silver enough to make me satisfactorily wealthy—and so my fancy was already busy with plans for spending this money. The first opportunity that offered, I sauntered carelessly away from the cabin, keeping an eye on the other boys, and stopping and con-

templating the sky when they seemed to be observing me; but as soon as the coast was manifestly
clear, I fled away as guiltily as a thief might have
done and never halted till I was far beyond sight
and call. Then I began my search with a feverish
excitement that was brimful of expectation — almost
of certainty. I crawled about the ground, seizing
and examining bits of stone, blowing the dust from
them or rubbing them on my clothes, and then
peering at them with anxious hope. Presently I
found a bright fragment and my heart bounded! I
hid behind a boulder and polished it and scrutinized
it with a nervous eagerness and a delight that was
more pronounced than absolute certainty itself could
have afforded. The more I examined the fragment
the more I was convinced that I had found the door
to fortune. I marked the spot and carried away my
specimen. Up and down the rugged mountain side
I searched, with always increasing interest and
always augmenting gratitude that I had come to
Humboldt and come in time. Of all the experiences
of my life, this secret search among the hidden
treasures of silver-land was the nearest to unmarred
ecstasy. It was a delirious revel. By and by, in
the bed of a shallow rivulet, I found a deposit of
shining yellow scales, and my breath almost forsook
me! A gold mine, and in my simplicity I had been
content with vulgar silver! I was so excited that I
half believed my overwrought imagination was
deceiving me. Then a fear came upon me that

people might be observing me and would guess my
secret.   Moved by this thought, I made a circuit of
the place, and ascended a knoll to reconnoiter.
Solitude.   No creature was near.   Then I returned
to my mine, fortifying myself against possible disappointment, but my fears were groundless — the
shining scales were still there.   I set about scooping
them out, and for an hour I toiled down the windings of the stream and robbed its bed.   But at last
the descending sun warned me to give up the quest,
and I turned homeward laden with wealth.   As I
walked along I could not help smiling at the thought
of my being so excited over my fragment of silver
when a nobler metal was almost under my nose.   In
this little time the former had so fallen in my esti-
mation that once or twice I was on the point of
throwing it away.

The boys were as hungry as usual, but I could
eat nothing.   Neither could I talk.   I was full of
dreams and far away.   Their conversation interrupted the flow of my fancy somewhat, and annoyed
me a little, too.   I despised the sordid and commonplace things they talked about.   But as they
proceeded, it began to amuse me.   It grew to be
rare fun to hear them planning their poor little
economies and sighing over possible privations and
distresses when a gold mine, all our own, lay within
sight of the cabin, and I could point it out at any
moment.   Smothered hilarity began to oppress me,
presently.   It was hard to resist the impulse to
15.

burst out with exultation and reveal everything; but
I did resist. I said within myself that I would filter
the great news through my lips calmly and be serene
as a summer morning while I watched its effect in
their faces. I said:

"Where have you all been?"

"Prospecting."

"What did you find?"

"Nothing."

"Nothing? What do you think of the country?"

"Can't tell, yet," said Mr. Ballou, who was an
old gold miner, and had likewise had considerable
experience among the silver mines.

"Well, haven't you formed any sort of opinion?"

"Yes, a sort of a one. It's fair enough here,
may be, but overrated. Seven-thousand-dollar
ledges are scarce, though. That Sheba may be rich
enough, but we don't own it; and besides, the rock
is so full of base metals that all the science in the
world can't work it. We'll not starve, here, but
we'll not get rich, I'm afraid."

"So you think the prospect is pretty poor?"

"No name for it!"

"Well, we'd better go back, hadn't we?"

"Oh, not yet—of course not. We'll try it a
riffle, first."

"Suppose, now—this is merely a supposition,
you know—suppose you could find a ledge that
would yield, say, a hundred and fifty dollars a ton
—would that satisfy you?"

" Try us once !" from the whole party.

" Or suppose — merely a supposition, of course — suppose you were to find a ledge that would yield two thousand dollars a ton — would *that* satisfy you?"

" Here — what do you mean? What are you coming at? Is there some mystery behind all this?"

" Never mind. I am not saying anything. You know perfectly well there are no rich mines here — of course you do. Because you have been around and examined for yourselves. Anybody would know that, that had been around. But just for the sake of argument, suppose — in a kind of general way — suppose some person were to tell you that two-thousand-dollar ledges were simply contemptible — contemptible, understand — and that right yonder in sight of this very cabin there were piles of pure gold and pure silver — oceans of it — enough to make you all rich in twenty-four hours ! Come !"

" I should say he was as crazy as a loon !" said old Ballou, but wild with excitement, nevertheless.

" Gentlemen," said I, " I don't say anything — *I* haven't been around, you know, and of course don't know anything — but all I ask of you is to cast your eye on *that*, for instance, and tell me what you think of it !" and I tossed my treasure before them.

There was an eager scramble for it, and a closing of heads together over it under the candle-light. Then old Ballou said:

o.

" Think of it? I think it is nothing but a lot of granite rubbish and nasty glittering mica that isn't worth ten cents an acre!"

So vanished my dream. So melted my wealth away. So toppled my airy castle to the earth and left me stricken and forlorn.

Moralizing, I observed, then, that " all that glitters is not gold."

Mr. Ballou said I could go further than that, and lay it up among my treasures of knowledge, that *nothing* that glitters is gold. So I learned then, once for all, that gold in its native state is but dull, unornamental stuff, and that only lowborn metals excite the admiration of the ignorant with an ostentatious glitter. However, like the rest of the world, I still go on underrating men of gold and glorifying men of mica. Commonplace human nature cannot rise above that.

CHAPTER XXIX.

TRUE knowledge of the nature of silver mining came fast enough. We went out "prospecting" with Mr. Ballou. We climbed the mountain sides, and clambered among sage-brush, rocks, and snow till we were ready to drop with exhaustion, but found no silver — nor yet any gold. Day after day we did this. Now and then we came upon holes burrowed a few feet into the declivities and apparently abandoned; and now and then we found one or two listless men still burrowing. But there was no appearance of silver. These holes were the beginnings of tunnels, and the purpose was to drive them hundreds of feet into the mountain, and some day tap the hidden ledge where the silver was. Some day! It seemed far enough away, and very hopeless and dreary. Day after day we toiled, and climbed, and searched, and we younger partners grew sicker and still sicker of the promiseless toil. At last we halted under a beetling rampart of rock which projected from the earth high upon the mountain. Mr. Ballou broke off some fragments with a hammer, and examined them long and atten-

tively with a small eyeglass; threw them away and
broke off more; said this rock was quartz, and
quartz was the sort of rock that contained silver.
Contained it! I had thought that at least it would
be caked on the outside of it like a kind of veneer-
ing. He still broke off pieces and critically examined them, now and then wetting the piece with
his tongue and applying the glass. At last he
exclaimed:

"We've got it!"

We were full of anxiety in a moment. The rock
was clean and white, where it was broken, and across
it ran a ragged thread of blue. He said that that
little thread had silver in it, mixed with base metals,
such as lead and antimony, and other rubbish, and
that there was a speck or two of gold visible. After
a great deal of effort we managed to discern some
little fine yellow specks, and judged that a couple
of tons of them massed together might make a gold
dollar, possibly. We were not jubilant, but Mr.
Ballou said there were worse ledges in the world
than that. He saved what he called the "richest"
piece of the rock, in order to determine its value by
the process called the "fire-assay." Then we
named the mine "Monarch of the Mountains"
(modesty of nomenclature is not a prominent feature
in the mines), and Mr. Ballou wrote out and stuck
up the following "notice," preserving a copy to be
entered upon the books in the mining recorder's
office in the town.

"NOTICE."

"We the undersigned claim three claims, of three hundred feet each (and one for discovery), on this silver-bearing quartz lead or lode, extending north and south from this notice, with all its dips, spurs, and angles, variations and sinuosities, together with fifty feet of ground on either side for working the same."

We put our names to it and tried to feel that our fortunes were made. But when we talked the matter all over with Mr. Ballou, we felt depressed and dubious. He said that this surface quartz was not all there was of our mine; but that the wall or ledge of rock called the "Monarch of the Mountains" extended down hundreds and hundreds of feet into the earth — he illustrated by saying it was like a curb-stone, and maintained a nearly uniform thickness — say twenty feet — away down into the bowels of the earth, and was perfectly distinct from the casing rock on each side of it; and that it kept to itself, and maintained its distinctive character always, no matter how deep it extended into the earth or how far it stretched itself through and across the hills and valleys. He said it might be a mile deep and ten miles long, for all we knew; and that wherever we bored into it above ground or below, we would find gold and silver in it, but no gold or silver in the meaner rock it was cased between. And he said that down in the great depths of the ledge was its richness, and the deeper it went the richer it grew. Therefore, instead of working here on the surface, we must either bore down into the rock with a shaft till we came to where it was

rich — say a hundred feet or so — or else we must
go down into the valley and bore a long tunnel into
the mountain side and tap the ledge far under the
earth. To do either was plainly the labor of
months; for we could blast and bore only a few feet
a day — some five or six. But this was not all.
He said that after we got the ore out it must be
hauled in wagons to a distant silver-mill, ground up,
and the silver extracted by a tedious and costly process. Our fortune seemed a century away!

But we went to work. We decided to sink a
shaft. So, for a week we climbed the mountain,
laden with picks, drills, gads, crowbars, shovels,
cans of blasting powder and coils of fuse, and strove
with might and main. At first the rock was broken
and loose, and we dug it up with picks and threw it
out with shovels, and the hole progressed very well.
But the rock became more compact, presently, and
gads and crowbars came into play. But shortly
nothing could make an impression but blasting
powder. That was the weariest work! One of us
held the iron drill in its place and another would
strike with an eight-pound sledge — it was like
driving nails on a large scale. In the course of an
hour or two the drill would reach a depth of two or
three feet, making a hole a couple of inches in
diameter. We would put in a charge of powder,
insert half a yard of fuse, pour in sand and gravel
and ram it down, then light the fuse and run.
When the explosion came and the rocks and smoke

shot into the air, we would go back and find about a bushel of that hard, rebellious quartz jolted out. Nothing more. One week of this satisfied me. I resigned. Clagget and Oliphant followed. Our shaft was only twelve feet deep. We decided that a tunnel was the thing we wanted.

So we went down the mountain side and worked a week; at the end of which time we had blasted a tunnel about deep enough to hide a hogshead in, and judged that about nine hundred feet more of it would reach the ledge. I resigned again, and the other boys only held out one day longer. We decided that a tunnel was not what we wanted. We wanted a ledge that was already "developed." There were none in the camp.

We dropped the "Monarch" for the time being. Meantime the camp was filling up with people, and there was a constantly growing excitement about our Humboldt mines. We fell victims to the epidemic and strained every nerve to acquire more "feet." We prospected and took up new claims, put "notices" on them and gave them grandiloquent names. We traded some of our "feet" for "feet" in other people's claims. In a little while we owned largely in the "Gray Eagle," the "Columbiana," the "Branch Mint," the "Maria Jane," the "Universe," the "Root-Hog-or-Die," the "Samson and Delilah," the "Treasure Trove," the "Golconda," the "Sultana," the "Boomerang," the "Great Republic," the "Grand Mogul," and fifty other

" mines" that had never been molested by a shovel
or scratched with a pick. We had not less than
thirty thousand "feet" apiece in the "richest
mines on earth" as the frenzied cant phrased it —
and were in debt to the butcher. We were stark
mad with excitement — drunk with happiness —
smothered under mountains of prospective wealth —
arrogantly compassionate toward the plodding
millions who knew not our marvelous canyon — but
our credit was not good at the grocer's.

It was the strangest phase of life one can imagine.
It was a beggars' revel. There was nothing doing
in the district — no mining — no milling — no pro-
ductive effort — no income — and not enough money
in the entire camp to buy a corner lot in an eastern
village, hardly; and yet a stranger would have supposed he was walking among bloated millionaires.
Prospecting parties swarmed out of town with the
first flush of dawn, and swarmed in again at nightfall laden with spoil — rocks. Nothing but rocks.
Every man's pockets were full of them; the floor of
his cabin was littered with them; they were disposed
in labeled rows on his shelves.

CHAPTER XXX.

I MET men at every turn who owned from one thousand to thirty thousand "feet" in undeveloped silver mines, every single foot of which they believed would shortly be worth from fifty to a thousand dollars — and as often as any other way they were men who had not twenty-five dollars in the world. Every man you met had his new mine to boast of, and his "specimens" ready; and if the opportunity offered, he would infallibly back you into a corner and offer as a favor to *you*, not to him, to part with just a few feet in the "Golden Age," or the "Sarah Jane," or some other unknown stack of croppings, for money enough to get a "square meal" with, as the phrase went. And you were never to reveal that he had made you the offer at such a ruinous price, for it was only out of friendship for you that he was willing to make the sacrifice. Then he would fish a piece of rock out of his pocket, and after looking mysteriously around as if he feared he might be waylaid and robbed if caught with such wealth in his possession, he would dab the rock against his tongue, clap an eyeglass to it, and exclaim:

16

"Look at that! Right there in that red dirt! See it? See the specks of gold? And the streak of silver? That's from the 'Uncle Abe.' There's a hundred thousand tons like that in sight! Right in sight, mind you! And when we get down on it and the ledge comes in solid, it will be the richest thing in the world! Look at the assay! I don't want you to believe *me* — look at the assay!"

Then he would get out a greasy sheet of paper which showed that the portion of rock assayed had given evidence of containing silver and gold in the proportion of so many hundreds or thousands of dollars to the ton. I little knew, then, that the custom was to hunt out the *richest* piece of rock and get it assayed! Very often, that piece, the size of a filbert, was the only fragment in a ton that had a particle of metal in it — and yet the assay made it pretend to represent the average value of the ton of rubbish it came from!

On such a system of assaying as that, the Humboldt world had gone crazy. On the authority of such assays its newspaper correspondents were frothing about rock worth four and seven thousand dollars a ton!

And does the reader remember, a few pages back, the calculations of a quoted correspondent, whereby the ore is to be mined and shipped all the way to England, the metals extracted, and the gold and silver contents received back by the miners as clear profit, the copper, antimony, and other things in

the ore being sufficient to pay all the expenses in-
curred? Everybody's head was full of such "calculations" as those — such raving insanity, rather. Few
people took *work* into their calculations — or outlay
of money either; except the work and expenditures
of other people.

We never touched our tunnel or our shaft again.
Why? Because we judged that we had learned the
real secret of success in silver mining — which was,
not to mine the silver ourselves by the sweat of our
brows and the labor of our hands, but to *sell* the ledges
to the dull slaves of toil and let them do the mining!

Before leaving Carson, the Secretary and I had
purchased "feet" from various Esmeralda stragglers. We had expected immediate returns of
bullion, but were only afflicted with regular and
constant "assessments" instead — demands for
money wherewith to develop the said mines. These
assessments had grown so oppressive that it seemed
necessary to look into the matter personally.
Therefore I projected a pilgrimage to Carson and
thence to Esmeralda. I bought a horse and started,
in company with Mr. Ballou and a gentleman named
Ollendorff, a Prussian — not the party who has inflicted so much suffering on the world with his
wretched foreign grammars, with their interminable
repetitions of questions which never have occurred
and are never likely to occur in any conversation
among human beings. We rode through a snow-
storm for two or three days, and arrived at " Honey

Lake Smith's," a sort of isolated inn on the Carson
river. It was a two-story log house situated on a
small knoll in the midst of the vast basin or desert
through which the sickly Carson winds its melancholy way. Close to the house were the Overland
stage stables, built of sun-dried bricks. There was
not another building within several leagues of the
place. Towards sunset about twenty hay-wagons
arrived and camped around the house, and all the
teamsters came in to supper — a very, very rough
set. There were one or two Overland stage-drivers
there, also, and half a dozen vagabonds and stragglers; consequently the house was well crowded.

We walked out, after supper, and visited a small
Indian camp in the vicinity. The Indians were in a
great hurry about something, and were packing up
and getting away as fast as they could. In their
broken English they said, " By'm-by, heap water!"
and by the help of signs made us understand that in
their opinion a flood was coming. The weather was
perfectly clear, and this was not the rainy season.
There was about a foot of water in the insignificant
river — or maybe two feet; the stream was not
wider than a back alley in a village, and its banks
were scarcely higher than a man's head. So, where
was the flood to come from? We canvassed the
subject awhile and then concluded it was a ruse, and
that the Indians had some better reason for leaving
in a hurry than fears of a flood in such an exceedingly dry time.

At seven in the evening we went to bed in the second story — with our clothes on, as usual, and all three in the same bed, for every available space on the floors, chairs, etc., were in request, and even then there was barely room for the housing of the inn's guests. An hour later we were awakened by a great turmoil, and springing out of bed we picked our way nimbly among the ranks of snoring teamsters on the floor and got to the front windows of the long room. A glance revealed a strange spectacle, under the moonlight. The crooked Carson was full to the brim, and its waters were raging and foaming in the wildest way — sweeping around the sharp bends at a furious speed, and bearing on their surface a chaos of logs, brush, and all sorts of rubbish. A depression, where its bed had once been, in other times, was already filling, and in one or two places the water was beginning to wash over the main bank. Men were flying hither and thither, bringing cattle and wagons close up to the house, for the spot of high ground on which it stood extended only some thirty feet in front and about a hundred in the rear. Close to the old river bed just spoken of, stood a little log stable, and in this our horses were lodged. While we looked, the waters increased so fast in this place that in a few minutes a torrent was roaring by the little stable and its margin encroaching steadily on the logs. We suddenly realized that this flood was not a mere holiday spectacle, but meant damage — and not only to the

small log stable, but to the Overland buildings close
to the main river, for the waves had now come ashore
and were creeping about the foundations and invading
the great hay-corral adjoining. We ran down and
joined the crowd of excited men and frightened
animals. We waded knee-deep into the log stable,
unfastened the horses and waded out almost *waist*-
deep, so fast the waters increased. Then the crowd
rushed in a body to the hay-corral and began to
tumble down the huge stacks of baled hay and roll
the bales up on the high ground by the house.
Meantime it was discovered that Owens, an Overland
driver, was missing, and a man ran to the large
stable, and wading in, boot-top deep, discovered
him asleep in his bed, awoke him, and waded out
again. But Owens was drowsy and resumed his
nap; but only for a minute or two, for presently he
turned in his bed, his hand dropped over the side
and came in contact with the cold water! It was
up level with the mattress! He waded out, breast-
deep, almost, and the next moment the sun-burned
bricks melted down like sugar and the big building
crumbled to a ruin and was washed away in a twinkling.

At eleven o'clock only the roof of the little log
stable was out of water, and our inn was on an island
in mid-ocean. As far as the eye could reach, in the
moonlight, there was no desert visible, but only a
level waste of shining water. The Indians were true
prophets, but how did they get their information?
I am not able to answer the question.

We remained cooped up eight days and nights with that curious crew. Swearing, drinking, and card-playing were the order of the day, and occasionally a fight was thrown in for variety. Dirt and vermin — but let us forget those features; their profusion is simply inconceivable — it is better that they remain so.

There were two men — however, this chapter is long enough.

16*

CHAPTER XXXI.

THERE were two men in the company who
caused me particular discomfort. One was a
little Swede, about twenty-five years old, who knew
only one song, and he was forever singing it. By
day we were all crowded into one small, stifling
barroom, and so there was no escaping this person's
music. Through all the profanity, whisky-guzzling,
" old sledge," and quarreling, his monotonous song
meandered with never a variation in its tiresome
sameness, and it seemed to me, at last, that I would
be content to die, in order to be rid of the torture.
The other man was a stalwart ruffian called " Arkansas," who carried two revolvers in his belt and a
bowie knife projecting from his boot, and who was
always drunk and always suffering for a fight. But
he was so feared, that nobody would accommodate
him. He would try all manner of little wary ruses
to entrap somebody into an offensive remark, and
his face would light up now and then when he
fancied he was fairly on the scent of a fight, but
invariably his victim would elude his toils and then
he would show a disappointment that was almost
pathetic. The landlord, Johnson, was a meek, well-

meaning fellow, and Arkansas fastened on him early, as a promising subject, and gave him no rest day or night, for awhile. On the fourth morning, Arkansas got drunk and sat himself down to wait for an opportunity. Presently Johnson came in, just comfortably sociable with whisky, and said:

"I reckon the Pennsylvania 'lection —"

Arkansas raised his finger impressively and Johnson stopped. Arkansas rose unsteadily and confronted him. Said he:

"Wha-what do you know a-about Pennsylvania? Answer me that. Wha-what do you know 'bout Pennsylvania?"

"I was only goin' to say —"

"You was only goin' to *say*. *You* was! You was only goin' to say — *what* was you goin' to say? That's it! That's what *I* want to know. *I* want to know wha-what you (*'ic*) what you know about Pennsylvania, since you're makin' yourself so d—d free. Answer me that!"

"Mr. Arkansas, if you'd only let me —"

"Who's a henderin' you? Don't you insinuate nothing agin me! — don't you do it. Don't you come in here bullyin' around, and cussin' and goin' on like a lunatic — don't you do it. 'Coz *I* won't *stand* it. If fight's what you want, out with it! I'm your man! Out with it!"

Said Johnson, backing into a corner, Arkansas following, menacingly:

"Why, *I* never said nothing, Mr. Arkansas.

P*

You don't give a man no chance. I was only goin'
to say that Pennsylvania was goin' to have an
election next week — that was all — that was everything I was goin' to say — I wish I may never stir if
it wasn't.''

" Well then why d'n't you say it? What did you
come swellin' around that way for, and tryin' to
raise trouble?''

"Why, *I* didn't come swellin' around, Mr.
Arkansas — I just —''

" I'm a liar am I! Ger-reat Cæsar's ghost —''

" Oh, please, Mr. Arkansas, I never meant such
a thing as that, I wish I may die if I did. All the
boys will tell you that I've always spoke well of
you, and respected you more'n any man in the
house. Ask Smith. Ain't it so, Smith? Didn't
I say, no longer ago than last night, that for a man
that was a gentleman *all* the time and every way you
took him, give me Arkansas? I'll leave it to any
gentleman here if them warn't the very words I
used. Come, now, Mr. Arkansas, le's take a drink
— le's shake hands and take a drink. Come up —
everybody! It's my treat. Come up, Bill, Tom,
Bob, Scotty — come up. I want you all to take a
drink with me and Arkansas — *old* Arkansas, I call
him — bully old Arkansas. Gimme your hand agin.
Look at him, boys — just take a *look* at him. Thar
stands the whitest man in America! — and the man
that denies it has got to fight *me*, that's all. Gimme
that old flipper agin!''

They embraced, with drunken affection on the landlord's part and unresponsive toleration on the part of Arkansas, who, bribed by a drink, was disappointed of his prey once more. But the foolish landlord was so happy to have escaped butchery, that he went on talking when he ought to have marched himself out of danger. The consequence was that Arkansas shortly began to glower upon him dangerously, and presently said:

"Lan'lord, will you p-please make that remark over agin if you please?"

"I was a-sayin' to Scotty that my father was up'ards of eighty year old when he died."

"Was that *all* that you said?"

"Yes, that was all."

"Didn't say nothing but that?"

"No — nothing."

Then an uncomfortable silence.

Arkansas played with his glass a moment, lolling on his elbows on the counter. Then he meditatively scratched his left shin with his right boot, while the awkward silence continued. But presently he loafed away toward the stove, looking dissatisfied; roughly shouldered two or three men out of a comfortable position; occupied it himself, gave a sleeping dog a kick that sent him howling under a bench, then spread his long legs and his blanket-coat tails apart and proceeded to warm his back. In a little while he fell to grumbling to himself, and soon he slouched back to the bar and said:

"Lan'lord, what's your idea for rakin' up old personalities and blowin' about your father? Ain't this company agreeable to you? Ain't it? If this company ain't agreeable to you, p'r'aps we'd better leave. Is that your idea? Is that what you're coming at?"

"Why bless your soul, Arkansas, I warn't thinking of such a thing. My father and my mother —"

"Lan'lord, *don't* crowd a man! Don't do it. If nothing'll do you but a disturbance, out with it like a man (*'ic*) — but *don't* rake up old bygones and fling 'em in the teeth of a passel of people that wants to be peaceable if they could git a chance. What's the matter with you this mornin', anyway? I never see a man carry on so."

"Arkansas, I reely didn't mean no harm, and I won't go on with it if it's onpleasant to you. I reckon my licker's got into my head, and what with the flood, and havin' so many to feed and look out for —"

"So *that's* what's a-ranklin' in your heart, is it? You want us to leave, do you? There's too many on us. You want us to pack up and swim. Is that it? Come!"

"Please be reasonable, Arkansas. Now *you* know that I ain't the man to —"

"Are you a threatenin' me? Are you? By George, the man don't live that can skeer me! Don't you try to come that game, my chicken — 'cuz I can stand a good deal, but I won't stand that.

Come out from behind that bar till I clean you!
You want to drive us out, do you, you sneakin'
underhanded hound! Come out from behind that
bar! *I'll* learn you to bully and badger and brow-
beat a gentleman that's forever trying to befriend
you and keep you out of trouble!''

" Please, Arkansas, please don't shoot! If there's
got to be bloodshed —''

" Do you hear that, gentlemen? Do you hear
him talk about bloodshed? So it's blood you want,
is it, you ravin' desperado! You'd made up your
mind to murder somebody this mornin'— I knowed
it perfectly well. I'm the man, am I? It's me
you're goin' to murder, is it? But you can't do it
'thout I get one chance first, you thievin' black-
hearted, white-livered son of a nigger! Draw your
weepon!''

With that, Arkansas began to shoot, and the
landlord to clamber over benches, men, and every
sort of obstacle in a frantic desire to escape. In
the midst of the wild hubbub the landlord crashed
through a glass door, and as Arkansas charged after
him the landlord's wife suddenly appeared in the
doorway and confronted the desperado with a pair
of scissors! Her fury was magnificent. With head
erect and flashing eye she stood a moment and then
advanced, with her weapon raised. The astonished
ruffian hesitated, and then fell back a step. She
followed. She backed him step by step into the
middle of the bar-room, and then, while the wonder-

ing crowd closed up and gazed, she gave him such another tongue-lashing as never a cowed and shame-faced braggart got before, perhaps! As she finished and retired victorious, a roar of applause shook the house, and every man ordered "drinks for the crowd" in one and the same breath.

The lesson was entirely sufficient. The reign of terror was over, and the Arkansas domination broken for good. During the rest of the season of island captivity, there was one man who sat apart in a state of permanent humiliation, never mixing in any quarrel or uttering a boast, and never resenting the insults the once cringing crew now constantly leveled at him, and that man was "Arkansas."

By the fifth or sixth morning the waters had sub-sided from the land, but the stream in the old river bed was still high and swift and there was no possi-bility of crossing it. On the eighth it was still too high for an entirely safe passage, but life in the inn had become next to insupportable by reason of the dirt, drunkenness, fighting, etc., and so we made an effort to get away. In the midst of a heavy snow-storm we embarked in a canoe, taking our saddles aboard and towing our horses after us by their halters. The Prussian, Ollendorff, was in the bow, with a paddle, Ballou paddled in the middle, and I sat in the stern holding the halters. When the horses lost their footing and began to swim, Ollen-dorff got frightened, for there was great danger that the horses would make our aim uncertain, and it was plain that if we failed to land at a certain spot the current would throw us off and almost surely cast us into the main Carson, which was a boiling torrent, now.   Such a catastrophe would be death, in all probability, for we would be swept to sea in the "Sink" or overturned and drowned. We warned Ollendorff to keep his wits about him and handle himself carefully, but it was useless; the moment the bow touched the bank, he made a spring and the canoe whirled upside down in ten-foot water. Ollendorff seized some brush and dragged himself ashore, but Ballou and I had to swim for it, encumbered with our overcoats.   But we held on to the canoe, and although we were washed down nearly to the Carson, we managed to push the boat ashore and make a safe landing. We were cold and water-soaked, but safe. The horses made a landing, too, but our saddles were gone, of course. We tied the animals in the sage-brush and there they had to stay for twenty-four hours. We baled out the canoe and ferried over some food and blankets for them, but we slept one more night in the inn before making another venture on our journey.

The next morning it was still snowing furiously when we got away with our new stock of saddles and accoutrements. We mounted and started. The snow lay so deep on the ground that there was no sign of a road perceptible, and the snow-fall was so thick that we could not see more than a hundred

yards ahead, else we could have guided our course
by the mountain ranges. The case looked dubious,
but Ollendorff said his instinct was as sensitive as
any compass, and that he could "strike a bee-line"
for Carson City and never diverge from it. He said
that if he were to straggle a single point out of the
true line his instinct would assail him like an outraged conscience. Consequently we dropped into
his wake happy and content. For half an hour we
poked along warily enough, but at the end of that
time we came upon a fresh trail, and Ollendorff
shouted proudly:

"I knew I was as dead certain as a compass,
boys! Here we are, right in somebody's tracks
that will hunt the way for us without any trouble,
Let's hurry up and join company with the party."

So we put the horses into as much of a trot as the
deep snow would allow, and before long it was
evident that we were gaining on our predecessors,
for the tracks grew more distinct. We hurried
along, and at the end of an hour the tracks looked
still newer and fresher — but what surprised us was,
that the *number* of travelers in advance of us
seemed to steadily increase. We wondered how so
large a party came to be travelling at such a time
and in such a solitude. Somebody suggested that
it must be a company of soldiers from the fort, and
so we accepted that solution and jogged along a little
faster still, for they could not be far off now. But
the tracks still multiplied, and we began to think the

platoon of soldiers was miraculously expanding into a regiment — Ballou said they had already increased to five hundred! Presently he stopped his horse and said:

"Boys, these are our own tracks, and we've actually been circussing round and round in a circle for more than two hours, out here in this blind desert! By George this is perfectly hydraulic!"

Then the old man waxed wroth and abusive. He called Ollendorff all manner of hard names — said he never saw such a lurid fool as he was, and ended with the peculiarly venomous opinion that he "did not know as much as a logarithm!"

We certainly had been following our own tracks. Ollendorff and his "mental compass" were in disgrace from that moment. After all our hard travel, here we were on the bank of the stream again, with the inn beyond dimly outlined through the driving snowfall. While we were considering what to do, the young Swede landed from the canoe and took his pedestrian way Carson-wards, singing his same tiresome song about his "sister and his brother" and "the child in the grave with its mother," and in a short minute faded and disappeared in the white oblivion. He was never heard of again. He no doubt got bewildered and lost, and Fatigue delivered him over to Sleep and Sleep betrayed him to Death. Possibly he followed our treacherous tracks till he became exhausted and dropped.

Presently the Overland stage forded the now fast

receding stream and started toward Carson on its
first trip since the flood came. We hesitated no
longer, now, but took up our march in its wake, and
trotted merrily along, for we had good confidence in
the driver's bump of locality. But our horses were
no match for the fresh stage team. We were soon
left out of sight; but it was no matter, for we had
the deep ruts the wheels made for a guide. By
this time it was three in the afternoon, and consequently it was not very long before night came —
and not with a lingering twilight, but with a sudden
shutting down like a cellar door, as is its habit in
that country. The snowfall was still as thick as ever,
and of course we could not see fifteen steps before
us; but all about us the white glare of the snow-
bed enabled us to discern the smooth sugar-loaf
mounds made by the covered sage-bushes, and just
in front of us the two faint grooves which we knew
were the steadily filling and slowly disappearing
wheel-tracks.

Now those sage-bushes were all about the same
height — three or four feet; they stood just about
seven feet apart, all over the vast desert; each of
them was a mere snow-mound, now; in *any* direction that you proceeded (the same as in a well-laid-
out orchard) you would find yourself moving down
a distinctly defined avenue, with a row of these
snow-mounds on either side of it — an avenue the
customary width of a road, nice and level in its
breadth, and rising at the sides in the most natural

way, by reason of the mounds. But we had not
thought of this. Then imagine the chilly thrill that
shot through us when it finally occurred to us, far in
the night, that since the last faint trace of the wheel-
tracks had long ago been buried from sight, we might
now be wandering down a mere sage-brush avenue,
miles away from the road and diverging further and
further away from it all the time. Having a cake
of ice slipped down one's back is placid comfort
compared to it. There was a sudden leap and stir
of blood that had been asleep for an hour, and as
sudden a rousing of all the drowsing activities in our
minds and bodies. We were alive and awake at
once — and shaking and quaking with consternation,
too. There was an instant halting and dismount-
ing, a bending low and an anxious scanning of the
road-bed. Useless, of course; for if a faint depression could not be discerned from an attitude of
four or five feet above it, it certainly could not with
one's nose nearly against it.

CHAPTER XXXII.

WE seemed to be in a road, but that was no
proof. We tested this by walking off in
various directions — the regular snow-mounds and
the regular avenues between them convinced each
man that *he* had found the true road, and that the
others had found only false ones. Plainly the
situation was desperate. We were cold and stiff
and the horses were tired. We decided to build a
sage-brush fire and camp out till morning. This
was wise, because if we were wandering from the
right road and the snow-storm continued another
day our case would be the next thing to hopeless if
we kept on.

All agreed that a camp fire was what would come
nearest to saving us, now, and so we set about building it. We could find no matches, and so we tried
to make shift with the pistols. Not a man in the
party had ever tried to do such a thing before, but
not a man in the party doubted that it *could* be
done, and without any trouble — because every man
in the party had read about it in books many a time
and had naturally come to believe it, with trusting

(254)

simplicity, just as he had long ago accepted and believed *that other* common book-fraud about Indians and lost hunters making a fire by rubbing two dry sticks together.

We huddled together on our knees in the deep snow, and the horses put their noses together and bowed their patient heads over us; and while the feathery flakes eddied down and turned us into a group of white statuary, we proceeded with the momentous experiment. We broke twigs from a sage-bush and piled them on a little cleared place in the shelter of our bodies. In the course of ten or fifteen minutes all was ready, and then, while conversation ceased and our pulses beat low with anxious suspense, Ollendorff applied his revolver, pulled the trigger and blew the pile clear out of the county! It was the flattest failure that ever was.

This was distressing, but it paled before a greater horror — the horses were gone! I had been appointed to hold the bridles, but in my absorbing anxiety over the pistol experiment I had unconsciously dropped them and the released animals had walked off in the storm. It was useless to try to follow them, for their footfalls could make no sound, and one could pass within two yards of the creatures and never see them. We gave them up without an effort at recovering them, and cursed the lying books that said horses would stay by their masters for protection and companionship in a distressful time like ours.

We were miserable enough, before; we felt still more forlorn, now. Patiently, but with blighted hope, we broke more sticks and piled them, and once more the Prussian shot them into annihilation. Plainly, to light a fire with a pistol was an art requiring practice and experience, and the middle of a desert at midnight in a snow-storm was not a good place or time for the acquiring of the accomplishment. We gave it up and tried the other. Each man took a couple of sticks and fell to chafing them together. At the end of half an hour we were thoroughly chilled, and so were the sticks. We bitterly execrated the Indians, the hunters, and the books that had betrayed us with the silly device, and wondered dismally what was next to be done. At this critical moment Mr. Ballou fished out four matches from the rubbish of an overlooked pocket. To have found four gold bars would have seemed poor and cheap good luck compared to this. One cannot think how good a match looks under such circumstances — or how lovable and precious, and sacredly beautiful to the eye. This time we gathered sticks with high hopes; and when Mr. Ballou prepared to light the first match, there was an amount of interest centered upon him that pages of writing could not describe. The match burned hopefully a moment, and then went out. It could not have carried more regret with it if it had been a human life. The next match simply flashed and died. The wind puffed the third one out just as it was on the imminent verge of success. We gathered together closer than ever, and developed a solicitude that was rapt and painful, as Mr. Ballou scratched our last hope on his leg. It lit, burned blue and sickly, and then budded into a robust flame. Shading it with his hands, the old gentleman bent gradually down and every heart went with him — everybody, too, for that matter — and blood and breath stood still. The flame touched the sticks at last, took gradual hold upon them — hesitated — took a stronger hold — hesitated again — held its breath five heart-breaking seconds, then gave a sort of human gasp, and went out.

Nobody said a word for several minutes. It was a solemn sort of silence; even the wind put on a stealthy, sinister quiet, and made no more noise than the falling flakes of snow. Finally a sad-voiced conversation began, and it was soon apparent that in each of our hearts lay the conviction that this was our last night with the living. I had so hoped that I was the only one who felt so. When the others calmly acknowledged their conviction, it sounded like the summons itself. Ollendorff said :

"Brothers, let us die together. And let us go without one hard feeling towards each other. Let us forget and forgive bygones. I know that you have felt hard towards me for turning over the canoe, and for knowing too much and leading you round and round in the snow — but I meant well;

17.

forgive me. I acknowledge freely that I have had hard feelings against Mr. Ballou for abusing me and calling me a logarithm, which is a thing I do not know what, but no doubt a thing considered disgraceful and unbecoming in America, and it has scarcely been out of my mind and has hurt me a great deal — but let it go; I forgive Mr. Ballou with all my heart, and —"

Poor Ollendorff broke down and the tears came. He was not alone, for I was crying too, and so was Mr. Ballou. Ollendorff got his voice again and forgave me for things I had done and said. Then he got out his bottle of whisky and said that whether he lived or died he would never touch another drop. He said he had given up all hope of life, and although ill-prepared, was ready to submit humbly to his fate; that he wished he could be spared a little longer, not for any selfish reason, but to make a thorough reform in his character, and by devoting himself to helping the poor, nursing the sick, and pleading with the people to guard themselves against the evils of intemperance, make his life a beneficent example to the young, and lay it down at last with the precious reflection that it had not been lived in vain. He ended by saying that his reform should begin at this moment, even here in the presence of death, since no longer time was to be vouchsafed wherein to prosecute it to men's help and benefit — and with that he threw away the bottle of whisky.

Mr. Ballou made remarks of similar purport, and

began the reform he could not live to continue, by throwing away the ancient pack of cards that had solaced our captivity during the flood and made it bearable. He said he never gambled, but still was satisfied that the meddling with cards in any way was immoral and injurious, and no man could be wholly pure and blemishless without eschewing them. "And therefore," continued he, " in doing this act I already feel more in sympathy with that spiritual saturnalia necessary to entire and obsolete reform." These rolling syllables touched him as no intelligible eloquence could have done, and the old man sobbed with a mournfulness not unmingled with satisfaction.

My own remarks were of the same tenor as those of my comrades, and I know that the feelings that prompted them were heartfelt and sincere. We were all sincere, and all deeply moved and earnest, for we were in the presence of death and without hope. I threw away my pipe, and in doing it felt that at last I was free of a hated vice and one that had ridden me like a tyrant all my days. While I yet talked, the thought of the good I might have done in the world, and the still greater good I might *now* do, with these new incentives and higher and better aims to guide me if I could only be spared a few years longer, overcame me and the tears came again. We put our arms about each other's necks and awaited the warning drowsiness that precedes death by freezing.

It came stealing over us presently, and then we

bade each other a last farewell.   A delicious dreami-
ness wrought its web about my yielding senses, while
the snow-flakes wove a winding sheet about my
conquered body.   Oblivion came.   The battle of
life was done.

CHAPTER XXXIII.

I DO not know how long I was in a state of forgetfulness, but it seemed an age. A vague consciousness grew upon me by degrees, and then came a gathering anguish of pain in my limbs and through all my body. I shuddered. The thought flitted through my brain, "this is death — this is the hereafter."

Then came a white upheaval at my side, and a voice said, with bitterness:

"Will some gentleman be so good as to kick me behind?"

It was Ballou — at least it was a towzled snow image in a sitting posture, with Ballou's voice.

I rose up, and there in the gray dawn, not fifteen steps from us, were the frame buildings of a stage station, and under a shed stood our still saddled and bridled horses!

An arched snow-drift broke up, now, and Ollendorff emerged from it, and the three of us sat and stared at the houses without speaking a word. We really had nothing to say. We were like the profane man who could not "do the subject justice," the

whole situation was so painfully ridiculous and humil-
iating that words were tame and we did not know
where to commence anyhow.

The joy in our hearts at our deliverance was
poisoned; well-nigh dissipated, indeed. We presently began to grow pettish by degrees, and sullen;
and then, angry at each other, angry at ourselves,
angry at everything in general, we moodily dusted
the snow from our clothing and in unsociable single
file plowed our way to the horses, unsaddled them,
and sought shelter in the station.

I have scarcely exaggerated a detail of this curious
and absurd adventure. It occurred almost exactly
as I have stated it. We actually went into camp in
a snow-drift in a desert, at midnight in a storm,
forlorn and hopeless, within fifteen steps of a comfortable inn.

For two hours we sat apart in the station and
ruminated in disgust. The mystery was gone, now,
and it was plain enough why the horses had deserted
us. Without a doubt they were under that shed a
quarter of a minute after they had left us, and
they must have overheard and enjoyed all our
confessions and lamentations.

After breakfast we felt better, and the zest of life
soon came back. The world looked bright again,
and existence was as dear to us as ever. Presently
an uneasiness came over me — grew upon me —
assailed me without ceasing. Alas, my regeneration
was not complete — I wanted to smoke! I resisted

RESURRECTED VICES

with all my strength, but the flesh was weak. I
wandered away alone and wrestled with myself an
hour. I recalled my promises of reform and
preached to myself persuasively, upbraidingly, ex-
haustively. But it was all vain, I shortly found myself sneaking among the snowdrifts hunting for my
pipe. I discovered it after a considerable search,
and crept away to hide myself and enjoy it. I remained behind the barn a good while, asking myself
how I would feel if my braver, stronger, truer comrades should catch me in my degradation. At last
I lit the pipe, and no human being can feel meaner
and baser than I did then. I was ashamed of being
in my own pitiful company. Still dreading discovery, I felt that perhaps the further side of the
barn would be somewhat safer, and so I turned the
corner. As I turned the one corner, smoking,
Ollendorff turned the other with his bottle to his lips,
and between us sat unconscious Ballou deep in a
game of " solitaire " with the old greasy cards!

Absurdity could go no farther. We shook hands
and agreed to say no more about " reform " and
" examples to the rising generation."

The station we were at was at the verge of the
Twenty-six Mile Desert. If we had approached it
half an hour earlier the night before, we must have
heard men shouting there and firing pistols; for
they were expecting some sheep drovers and their
flocks and knew that they would infallibly get lost
and wander out of reach of help unless guided by

sounds. While we remained at the station, three of the drovers arrived, nearly exhausted with their wanderings, but two others of their party were never heard of afterward.

We reached Carson in due time, and took a rest. This rest, together with preparations for the journey to Esmeralda, kept us there a week, and the delay gave us the opportunity to be present at the trial of the great landslide case of Hyde *vs*. Morgan — an episode which is famous in Nevada to this day. After a word or two of necessary explanation, I will set down the history of this singular affair just as it transpired.

CHAPTER XXXIV.

THE mountains are very high and steep about Carson, Eagle, and Washoe Valleys — very high and very steep, and so when the snow gets to melting off fast in the spring and the warm surface-earth begins to moisten and soften, the disastrous landslides commence. The reader cannot know what a landslide is, unless he has lived in that country and seen the whole side of a mountain taken off some fine morning and deposited down in the valley, leaving a vast, treeless, unsightly scar upon the mountain's front to keep the circumstance fresh in his memory all the years that he may go on living within seventy miles of that place.

General Buncombe was shipped out to Nevada in the invoice of Territorial officers, to be United States Attorney. He considered himself a lawyer of parts, and he very much wanted an opportunity to mani-fest it — partly for the pure gratification of it and partly because his salary was Territorially meager (which is a strong expression). Now the older citi-zens of a new Territory look down upon the rest of the world with a calm, benevolent compassion, as long as it keeps out of the way — when it gets in the way they snub it. Sometimes this latter takes the shape of a practical joke.

One morning Dick Hyde rode furiously up to General Buncombe's door in Carson City and rushed into his presence without stopping to tie his horse. He seemed much excited. He told the General that he wanted him to conduct a suit for him and would pay him five hundred dollars if he achieved a victory. And then, with violent gestures and a world of profanity, he poured out his griefs. He said it was pretty well known that for some years he had been farming (or ranching as the more customary term is) in Washoe District, and making a successful thing of it, and furthermore it was known that his ranch was situated just in the edge of the valley, and that Tom Morgan owned a ranch immediately above it on the mountain side. And now the trouble was, that one of those hated and dreaded landslides had come and slid Morgan's ranch, fences, cabins, cattle, barns, and everything down on top of *his* ranch and exactly covered up every single vestige of his property, to a depth of about thirty-eight feet. Morgan was in possession and refused to vacate the premises — said he was occupying his own cabin and not interfering with anybody else's — and said the cabin was standing on the same dirt and same ranch it had always stood on, and he would like to see anybody make him vacate.

"And when I reminded him," said Hyde, weep-

ing, "that it was on top of my ranch and that he
was trespassing, he had the infernal meanness to ask
me why didn't I *stay* on my ranch and hold possession when I see him a-coming! Why didn't I *stay*
on it, the blathering lunatic — by George, when I
heard that racket and looked up that hill it was just
like the whole world was a-ripping and a-tearing
down that mountain side — splinters and cord-
wood, thunder and lightning, hail and snow, odds
and ends of haystacks, and awful clouds of dust!
— trees going end over end in the air, rocks as big
as a house jumping 'bout a thousand feet high and
busting into ten million pieces, cattle turned inside
out and a-coming head on with their tails hanging out
between their teeth! — and in the midst of all that
wrack and destruction sot that cussed Morgan on his
gatepost, a-wondering why I didn't *stay and hold
possession!* Laws bless me, I just took one glimpse,
General, and lit out'n the county in three jumps
exactly.

"But what grinds me is that that Morgan hangs
on there and won't move off'n that ranch — says it's
his'n and he's going to keep it — likes it better'n he
did when it was higher up the hill. Mad! Well,
I've been so mad for two days I couldn't find my
way to town — been wandering around in the brush
in a starving condition — got anything here to drink,
General? But I'm here *now*, and I'm a-going to
law. You hear *me!*"

Never in all the world, perhaps, were a man's feel-
18

*ings so outraged as were the General's. He said he
had never heard of such high-handed conduct in all
his life as this Morgan's. And he said there was no
use in going to law — Morgan had no shadow of right
to remain where he was — nobody in the wide world
would uphold him in it, and no lawyer would take
his case and no judge listen to it. Hyde said that
right there was where he was mistaken — everybody
in town sustained Morgan; Hal Brayton, a very
smart lawyer, had taken his case; the courts being
in vacation, it was to be tried before a referee, and
ex-Governor Roop had already been appointed to
that office, and would open his court in a large public
hall near the hotel at two that afternoon.

The General was amazed. He said he had suspected before that the people of that Territory were
fools, and now he knew it. But he said rest easy,
rest easy and collect the witnesses, for the victory
was just as certain as if the conflict were already
over. Hyde wiped away his tears and left.

At two in the afternoon referee Roop's Court
opened, and Roop appeared throned among his
sheriffs, the witnesses, and spectators, and wearing
upon his face a solemnity so awe-inspiring that some
of his fellow-conspirators had misgivings that maybe
he had not comprehended, after all, that this was
merely a joke. An unearthly stillness prevailed, for
at the slightest noise the judge uttered sternly the
command:

" Order in the Court!"

And the sheriffs promptly echoed it. Presently the General elbowed his way through the crowd of spectators, with his arms full of law-books, and on his ears fell an order from the judge which was the first respectful recognition of his high official dignity that had ever saluted them, and it trickled pleasantly through his whole system:

"Way for the United States Attorney!"

The witnesses were called — legislators, high government officers, ranchmen, miners, Indians, Chinamen, negroes. Three-fourths of them were called by the defendant Morgan, but no matter, their testimony invariably went in favor of the plaintiff Hyde. Each new witness only added new testimony to the absurdity of a man's claiming to own another man's property because his farm had slid down on top of it. Then the Morgan lawyers made their speeches, and seemed to make singularly weak ones — they did really nothing to help the Morgan cause. And now the General, with exultation in his face, got up and made an impassioned effort; he pounded the table, he banged the law-books, he shouted, and roared, and howled, he quoted from everything and everybody, poetry, sarcasm, statistics, history, pathos, bathos, blasphemy, and wound up with a grand war-whoop for free speech, freedom of the press, free schools, the Glorious Bird of America and the principles of eternal justice! [Applause.]

When the General sat down, he did it with the conviction that if there was anything in good strong testimony, a great speech and believing and admiring countenances all around, Mr. Morgan's case was killed. Ex-Governor Roop leant his head upon his hand for some minutes, thinking, and the still audience waited for his decision. And then he got up and stood erect, with bended head, and thought again. Then he walked the floor with long, deliberate strides, his chin in his hand, and still the audience waited. At last he returned to his throne, seated himself, and began, impressively:

"Gentlemen, I feel the great responsibility that rests upon me this day. This is no ordinary case. On the contrary, it is plain that it is the most solemn and awful that ever man was called upon to decide. Gentlemen, I have listened attentively to the evidence, and have perceived that the weight of it, the overwhelming weight of it, is in favor of the plaintiff Hyde. I have listened also to the remarks of counsel, with high interest — and especially will I commend the masterly and irrefutable logic of the distinguished gentleman who represents the plaintiff. But, gentlemen, let us beware how we allow mere human testimony, human ingenuity in argument and human ideas of equity, to influence us at a moment so solemn as this. Gentlemen, it ill becomes us, worms as we are, to meddle with the decrees of Heaven. It is plain to me that Heaven, in its inscrutable wisdom, has seen fit to move this defendant's ranch for a purpose. We are but creatures, and we must submit. If Heaven has chosen to favor the defendant Morgan in this marked and wonderful manner; and if Heaven, dissatisfied with the position of the Morgan ranch upon the mountain side, has chosen to remove it to a position more eligible and more advantageous for its owner, it ill becomes us, insects as we are, to question the legality of the act or inquire into the reasons that prompted it. No — Heaven created the ranches, and it is Heaven's prerogative to rearrange them, to experiment with them, to shift them around at its pleasure. It is for us to submit, without repining. I warn you that this thing which has happened is a thing with which the sacrilegious hands and brains and tongues of men must not meddle. Gentlemen, it is the verdict of this court that the plaintiff, Richard Hyde, has been deprived of his ranch by the visitation of God! And from this decision there is no appeal."

Buncombe seized his cargo of law-books and plunged out of the court-room frantic with indignation. He pronounced Roop to be a miraculous fool, an inspired idiot. In all good faith he returned at night and remonstrated with Roop upon his extravagant decision, and implored him to walk the floor and think for half an hour, and see if he could not figure out some sort of modification of the verdict. Roop yielded at last and got up to walk. He walked two hours and a half, and at last his face lit up happily and he told Buncombe it had occurred to him that the ranch underneath the new Morgan ranch still belonged to Hyde, that his title to the ground

was just as good as it had ever been, and therefore
he was of opinion that Hyde had a right to dig it out
from under there and—

The General never waited to hear the end of it.
He was always an impatient and irascible man,
that way.   At the end of two months the fact that
he had been played upon with a joke had managed
to bore itself, like another Hoosac Tunnel, through
the solid adamant of his understanding.

CHAPTER XXXV.

WHEN we finally left for Esmeralda, horseback, we had an addition to the company in the person of Capt. John Nye, the Governor's brother. He had a good memory, and a tongue hung in the middle. This is a combination which gives immortality to conversation. Capt. John never suffered the talk to flag or falter once during the hundred and twenty miles of the journey. In addition to his conversational powers, he had one or two other endowments of a marked character. One was a singular "handiness" about doing anything and everything, from laying out a railroad or organizing a political party, down to sewing on buttons, shoeing a horse, or setting a broken leg, or a hen. Another was a spirit of accommodation that prompted him to take the needs, difficulties, and perplexities of anybody and everybody upon his own shoulders at any and all times, and dispose of them with admirable facility and alacrity — hence he always managed to find vacant beds in crowded inns, and plenty to eat in the emptiest larders. And finally, wherever he met a man, woman or child, in

18*   (273)

camp, inn, or desert, he either knew such parties
personally or had been acquainted with a relative of
the same. Such another traveling comrade was
never seen before. I cannot forbear giving a specimen of the way in which he overcame difficulties.
On the second day out, we arrived, very tired and
hungry, at a poor little inn in the desert, and were
told that the house was full, no provisions on hand,
and neither hay nor barley to spare for the horses —
we must move on. The rest of us wanted to hurry
on while it was yet light, but Capt. John insisted on
stopping awhile. We dismounted and entered. There
was no welcome for us on any face. Capt. John began his blandishments, and within twenty minutes he
had accomplished the following things, viz.: found
old acquaintances in three teamsters; discovered that
he used to go to school with the landlord's mother;
recognized his wife as a lady whose life he had saved
once in California, by stopping her runaway horse;
mended a child's broken toy and won the favor of
its mother, a guest of the inn; helped the hostler
bleed a horse, and prescribed for another horse that
had the " heaves "; treated the entire party three
times at the landlord's bar; produced a later paper
than anybody had seen for a week and sat himself
down to read the news to a deeply-interested audience. The result, summed up, was as follows: The
hostler found plenty of feed for our horses; we had
a trout supper, an exceedingly sociable time after it,
good beds to sleep in, and a surprising breakfast in

the morning — and when we left, we left lamented by all! Capt. John had some bad traits, but he had some uncommonly valuable ones to offset them with.

Esmeralda was in many respects another Humboldt, but in a little more forward state. The claims we had been paying assessments on were entirely worthless, and we threw them away. The principal one cropped out of the top of a knoll that was fourteen feet high, and the inspired Board of Directors were running a tunnel under that knoll to strike the ledge. The tunnel would have to be seventy feet long, and would then strike the ledge at the same depth that a *shaft* twelve feet deep would have reached! The Board were living on the "assessments." [N. B. — This hint comes too late for the enlightenment of New York silver miners; they have already learned all about this neat trick by experience.] The Board had no desire to strike the ledge, knowing that it was as barren of silver as a curbstone. This reminiscence calls to mind Jim Townsend's tunnel. He had paid assessments on a mine called the "Daley" till he was well-nigh penniless. Finally an assessment was levied to run a tunnel two hundred and fifty feet on the Daley, and Townsend went up on the hill to look into matters. He found the Daley cropping out of the apex of an exceedingly sharp-pointed peak, and a couple of men up there "facing" the proposed tunnel. Townsend made a calculation. Then he said to the men:

R.

"So you have taken a contract to run a tunnel into this hill two hundred and fifty feet to strike this ledge?"

"Yes, sir."

"Well, do you know that you have got one of the most expensive and arduous undertakings before you that was ever conceived by man?"

"Why no — how is that?"

"Because this hill is only twenty-five feet through from side to side; and so you have got to build two hundred and twenty-five feet of your tunnel on trestle-work!"

The ways of silver mining Boards are exceedingly dark and sinuous.

We took up various claims, and *commenced* shafts and tunnels on them, but never finished any of them. We had to do a certain amount of work on each to "hold" it, else other parties could seize our property after the expiration of ten days. We were always hunting up new claims and doing a little work on them and then waiting for a buyer — who never came. We never found any ore that would yield more than fifty dollars a ton; and as the mills charged fifty dollars a ton for *working* ore and extracting the silver, our pocket-money melted steadily away and none returned to take its place. We lived in a little cabin and cooked for ourselves; and altogether it was a hard life, though a hopeful one — for we never ceased to expect fortune and a customer to burst upon us some day.

At last, when flour reached a dollar a pound, and money could not be borrowed on the best security at less than *eight per cent. a month* (I being without the security, too), I abandoned mining and went to milling.   That is to say, I went to work as a common laborer in a quartz mill, at ten dollars a week and board.

CHAPTER XXXVI.

I HAD already learned how hard and long and dismal a task it is to burrow down into the bowels of the earth and get out the coveted ore; and now I learned that the burrowing was only half the work; and that to get the silver out of the ore was the dreary and laborious other half of it. We had to turn out at six in the morning and keep at it till dark. This mill was a six-stamp affair, driven by steam. Six tall, upright rods of iron, as large as a man's ankle, and heavily shod with a mass of iron and steel at their lower ends, were framed together like a gate, and these rose and fell, one after the other, in a ponderous dance, in an iron box called a "battery." Each of these rods or stamps weighed six hundred pounds. One of us stood by the battery all day long, breaking up masses of silver-bearing rock with a sledge and shoveling it into the battery. The ceaseless dance of the stamps pulverized the rock to powder, and a stream of water that trickled into the battery turned it to a creamy paste. The minutest particles were driven through a fine wire screen which fitted close around

the battery, and were washed into great tubs warmed
by superheated steam — amalgamating pans, they
are called. The mass of pulp in the pans was kept
constantly stirred up by revolving "mullers." A
quantity of quicksilver was kept always in the battery, and this seized some of the liberated gold and
silver particles and held on to them; quicksilver was
shaken in a fine shower into the pans, also, about
every half hour, through a buckskin sack. Quantities of coarse salt and sulphate of copper were
added, from time to time to assist the amalgamation
by destroying base metals which coated the gold
and silver and would not let it unite with the quicksilver. All these tiresome things we had to attend
to constantly. Streams of dirty water flowed always
from the pans and were carried off in broad wooden
troughs to the ravine. One would not suppose that
atoms of gold and silver would float on top of six
inches of water, but they did; and in order to catch
them, coarse blankets were laid in the troughs, and
little obstructing "riffles" charged with quicksilver
were placed here and there across the troughs also.
These riffles had to be cleaned and the blankets
washed out every evening, to get their precious accumulations — and after all this eternity of trouble
one-third of the silver and gold in a ton of rock
would find its way to the end of the troughs in the
ravine at last and have to be worked over again
some day. There is nothing so aggravating as
silver milling. There never was any idle time in

that mill. There was always something to do. It
is a pity that Adam could not have gone straight
out of Eden into a quartz mill, in order to understand
the full force of his doom to " earn his bread by the
sweat of his brow." Every now and then, during
the day, we had to scoop some pulp out of the
pans, and tediously " wash " it in a horn spoon —
wash it little by little over the edge till at last nothing was left but some little dull globules of quicksilver in the bottom. If they were soft and yielding, the pan needed some salt or some sulphate of
copper or some other chemical rubbish to assist
digestion; if they were crisp to the touch and would
retain a dint, they were freighted with all the silver
and gold they could seize and hold, and consequently the pans needed a fresh charge of quicksilver. When there was nothing else to do, one
could always " screen tailings." That is to say, he
could shovel up the dried sand that had washed
down to the ravine through the troughs and dash it
against an upright wire screen to free it from peb-
bles and prepare it for working over. The process
of amalgamation differed in the various mills, and
this included changes in style of pans and other
machinery, and a great diversity of opinion existed
as to the best in use, but none of the methods employed involved the principle of milling ore without " screening the tailings." Of all recreations in
the world, screening tailings on a hot day, with a
long-handled shovel, is the most undesirable.

At the end of the week the machinery was stopped and we "cleaned up." That is to say, we got the pulp out of the pans and batteries, and washed the mud patiently away till nothing was left but the long accumulating mass of quicksilver, with its imprisoned treasures. This we made into heavy, compact snowballs, and piled them up in a bright, luxurious heap for inspection. Making these snowballs cost me a fine gold ring — that and ignorance together; for the quicksilver invaded the ring with the same facility with which water saturates a sponge — separated its particles and the ring crumbled to pieces.

We put our pile of quicksilver balls into an iron retort that had a pipe leading from it to a pail of water, and then applied a roasting heat. The quicksilver turned to vapor, escaped through the pipe into the pail, and the water turned it into good wholesome quicksilver again. Quicksilver is very costly, and they never waste it. On opening the retort, there was our week's work — a lump of pure white, frosty looking silver, twice as large as a man's head. Perhaps a fifth of the mass was gold, but the color of it did not show — would not have shown if two-thirds of it had been gold. We melted it up and made a solid brick of it by pouring it into an iron brick-mold.

By such a tedious and laborious process were silver bricks obtained. This mill was but one of many others in operation at the time. The first one in Nevada was built at Egan Canyon and was a small insignificant affair and compared most unfavorably with some of the immense establishments afterward located at Virginia City and elsewhere.

From our bricks a little corner was chipped off for the " fire assay "— a method used to determine the proportions of gold, silver, and base metals in the mass. This is an interesting process. The chip is hammered out as thin as paper and weighed on scales so fine and sensitive that if you weigh a two-inch scrap of paper on them and then write your name on the paper with a coarse, soft pencil and weigh it again, the scales will take marked notice of the addition. Then a little lead (also weighed) is rolled up with the flake of silver, and the two are melted at a great heat in a small vessel called a cupel, made by compressing bone ashes into a cup-shape in a steel mold. The base metals oxydize and are absorbed with the lead into the pores of the cupel. A button or globule of perfectly pure gold and silver is left behind, and by weighing it and noting the loss, the assayer knows the proportion of base metal the brick contains. He has to separate the gold from the silver now. The button is hammered out flat and thin, put in the furnace and kept some time at a red heat; after cooling it off it is rolled up like a quill and heated in a glass vessel containing nitric acid; the acid dissolves the silver and leaves the gold pure and ready to be weighed on its own merits. Then salt water is poured into the vessel containing the dissolved silver, and the silver returns to palpable form again and sinks to the bottom. Nothing now remains but to weigh it; then the proportions of the several metals contained in the brick are known, and the assayer stamps the value of the brick upon its surface.

The sagacious reader will know now, without being told, that the speculative miner, in getting a "fire-assay" made of a piece of rock from his mine (to help him sell the same), was not in the habit of picking out the least valuable fragment of rock on his dump-pile, but quite the contrary. I have seen men hunt over a pile of nearly worthless quartz for an hour, and at last find a little piece as large as a filbert, which was rich in gold and silver — and this was reserved for a fire-assay! Of course the fire-assay would demonstrate that a ton of such rock would yield hundreds of dollars — and on such assays many an utterly worthless mine was sold.

Assaying was a good business, and so some men engaged in it, occasionally, who were not strictly scientific and capable. One assayer got such rich results out of all specimens brought to him that in time he acquired almost a monopoly of the business But like all men who achieve success, he became an object of envy and suspicion. The other assayers entered into a conspiracy against him, and let some prominent citizens into the secret in order to show that they meant fairly. Then they broke a little fragment off a carpenter's grindstone and got a stranger to take it to the popular scientist and get it assayed. In the course of an hour the result came — whereby it appeared that a ton of that rock would yield $1,284.40 in silver and $366.36 in gold!

Due publication of the whole matter was made in the paper, and the popular assayer left town " between two days."

I will remark, in passing, that I only remained in the milling business one week. I told my employer I could not stay longer without an advance in my wages; that I liked quartz milling, indeed was infatuated with it; that I had never before grown so tenderly attached to an occupation in so short a time; that nothing, it seemed to me, gave such scope to intellectual activity as feeding a battery and screening tailings, and nothing so stimulated the moral attributes as retorting bullion and washing blankets — still, I felt constrained to ask an increase of salary.

He said he was paying me ten dollars a week, and thought it a good round sum. How much did I want?

I said about four hundred thousand dollars a month, and board, was about all I could reasonably ask, considering the hard times.

I was ordered off the premises! And yet, when I look back to those days and call to mind the exceeding hardness of the labor I performed in that mill, I only regret that I did not ask him seven hundred thousand.

Shortly after this I began to grow crazy, along with the rest of the population, about the mysterious and wonderful " cement mine," and to make preparations to take advantage of any opportunity that might offer to go and help hunt for it.

CHAPTER XXXVII.

IT was somewhere in the neighborhood of Mono Lake that the marvelous Whiteman cement mine was supposed to lie. Every now and then it would be reported that Mr. W. had passed stealthily through Esmeralda at dead of night, in disguise, and then we would have a wild excitement — because he must be steering for his secret mine, and now was the time to follow him. In less than three hours after daylight all the horses and mules and donkeys in the vicinity would be bought, hired, or stolen, and half the community would be off for the mountains, following in the wake of Whiteman. But W. would drift about through the mountain gorges for days together, in a purposeless sort of way, until the provisions of the miners ran out, and they would have to go back home. I have known it reported at eleven at night, in a large mining camp, that Whiteman had just passed through, and in two hours the streets, so quiet before, would be swarming with men and animals. Every individual would be trying to be very secret, but yet venturing to whisper to just one neighbor that W. had passed

through.   And long before daylight — this in the
dead of winter — the stampede would be complete,
the camp deserted, and the whole population gone
chasing after W.

The tradition was that in the early immigration,
more than twenty years ago, three young Germans,
brothers, who had survived an Indian massacre on
the Plains, wandered on foot through the deserts,
avoiding all trails and roads, and simply holding a
westerly direction and hoping to find California before they starved or died of fatigue.   And in a
gorge in the mountains they sat down to rest one
day, when one of them noticed a curious vein of
cement running along the ground, shot full of lumps
of dull yellow metal.   They saw that it was gold,
and that here was a fortune to be acquired in a single
day.   The vein was about as wide as a curbstone,
and fully two-thirds of it was pure gold.   Every
pound of the wonderful cement was worth wellnigh
$200.   Each of the brothers loaded himself with
about twenty-five pounds of it, and then they covered up all traces of the vein, made a rude drawing
of the locality and the principal landmarks in the
vicinity, and started westward again.   But troubles
thickened about them.   In their wanderings one
brother fell and broke his leg, and the others were
obliged to go on and leave him to die in the wilderness.   Another worn out and starving, gave up by
and by, and laid down to die, but after two or three
weeks of incredible hardships, the third reached the

settlements of California exhausted, sick, and his
mind deranged by his sufferings. He had throwr
away all his cement but a few fragments, but thes:
were sufficient to set everybody wild with excitement. However, he had had enough of the cement
country, and nothing could induce him to lead a
party thither. He was entirely content to work on
a farm for wages. But he gave Whiteman his map,
and described the cement region as well as he could,
and thus transferred the curse to that gentleman —
for when I had my one accidental glimpse of Mr.
W. in Esmeralda he had been hunting for the lost
mine, in hunger and thirst, poverty and sickness,
for twelve or thirteen years. Some people believed
he had found it, but most people believed he had
not. I saw a piece of cement as large as my fist
which was said to have been given to Whiteman by
the young German, and it was of a seductive nature.
Lumps of virgin gold were as thick in it as raisins in
a slice of fruit cake. The privilege of working such
a mine one week would be sufficient for a man of
reasonable desires.

A new partner of ours, a Mr. Higbie, knew
Whiteman well by sight, and a friend of ours, a Mr.
Van Dorn, was well acquainted with him, and not
only that, but had Whiteman's promise that he
should have a private hint in time to enable him to
join the next cement expedition. Van Dorn had
promised to extend the hint to us. One evening
Higbie came in greatly excited, and said he felt

certain he had recognized Whiteman, up town, dis-
guised and in a pretended state of intoxication. In
a little while Van Dorn arrived and confirmed the
news; and so we gathered in our cabin and with
heads close together arranged our plans in impressive
whispers.

We were to leave town quietly, after midnight, in
two or three small parties, so as not to attract attention, and meet at dawn on the "divide" overlooking Mono Lake, eight or nine miles distant. We
were to make no noise after starting, and not speak
above a whisper under any circumstances. It was
believed that for once Whiteman's presence was unknown in the town and his expedition unsuspected.
Our conclave broke up at nine o'clock, and we set
about our preparations diligently and with profound
secrecy. At eleven o'clock we saddled our horses,
hitched them with their long *riatas* (or lassos), and
then brought out a side of bacon, a sack of beans, a
small sack of coffee, some sugar, a hundred pounds
of flour in sacks, some tin cups and a coffee-pot,
frying pan and some few other necessary articles.
All these things were "packed" on the back of a
led horse — and whoever has not been taught, by a
Spanish adept, to pack an animal, let him never
hope to do the thing by natural smartness. That is
impossible. Higbie had had some experience, but
was not perfect. He put on the pack saddle (a
thing like a sawbuck), piled the property on it, and
then wound a rope all over and about it and under

19.

it, "every which way," taking a hitch in it every now and then, and occasionally surging back on it till the horse's side sunk in and he gasped for breath — but every time the lashings grew tight in one place they loosened in another. We never did get the load tight all over, but we got it so that it would do, after a fashion, and then we started, in single file, close order, and without a word. It was a dark night. We kept the middle of the road, and proceeded in a slow walk past the rows of cabins, and whenever a miner came to his door I trembled for fear the light would shine on us and excite curiosity. But nothing happened. We began the long winding ascent of the canyon, toward the "divide," and presently the cabins began to grow infrequent, and the intervals between them wider and wider, and then I began to breathe tolerably freely and feel less like a thief and a murderer. I was in the rear, leading the pack horse. As the ascent grew steeper he grew proportionately less satisfied with his cargo, and began to pull back on his *riata* occasionally and delay progress. My comrades were passing out of sight in the gloom. I was getting anxious. I coaxed and bullied the pack horse till I presently got him into a trot, and then the tin cups and pans strung about his person frightened him and he ran. His *riata* was wound around the pommel of my saddle, and so, as he went by he dragged me from my horse and the two animals traveled briskly on without me. But I was not alone — the loosened cargo tumbled overboard from the pack horse and fell close to me. It was abreast of almost the last cabin. A miner came out and said:

"Hello!"

I was thirty steps from him, and knew he could not see me, it was so very dark in the shadow of the mountain. So I lay still. Another head appeared in the light of the cabin door, and presently the two men walked toward me. They stopped within ten steps of me, and one said:

"'St! Listen."

I could not have been in a more distressed state if I had been escaping justice with a price on my head. Then the miners appeared to sit down on a boulder, though I could not see them distinctly enough to be very sure what they did. One said:

"I heard a noise, as plain as I ever heard anything. It seemed to be about there—"

A stone whizzed by my head. I flattened myself out in the dust like a postage stamp, and thought to myself if he mended his aim ever so little he would probably hear another noise. In my heart, now, I execrated secret expeditions. I promised myself that this should be my last, though the Sierras were ribbed with cement veins. Then one of the men said:

"I'll tell you what! Welch knew what he was talking about when he said he saw Whiteman to-day. I heard horses — that was the noise. I am going down to Welch's, right away."

They left and I was glad. I did not care whither they went, so they went. I was willing they should visit Welch, and the sooner the better.

As soon as they closed their cabin door my comrades emerged from the gloom; they had caught the horses and were waiting for a clear coast again. We remounted the cargo on the pack horse and got under way, and as day broke we reached the "divide" and joined Van Dorn. Then we journeyed down into the valley of the lake, and feeling secure, we halted to cook breakfast, for we were tired and sleepy and hungry. Three hours later the rest of the population filed over the "divide" in a long procession, and drifted off out of sight around the borders of the lake!

Whether or not my accident had produced this result we never knew, but at least one thing was certain — the secret was out and Whiteman would not enter upon a search for the cement mine this time. We were filled with chagrin.

We held a council and decided to make the best of our misfortune and enjoy a week's holiday on the borders of the curious lake. Mono, it is sometimes called, and sometimes the "Dead Sea of California." It is one of the strangest freaks of Nature to be found in any land, but it is hardly ever mentioned in print and very seldom visited, because it lies away off the usual routes of travel, and besides is so difficult to get at that only men content to endure the roughest life will consent to take upon themselves the discomforts of such a trip. On the morning of our second day, we traveled around to a remote and particularly wild spot on the borders of the lake, where a stream of fresh, ice-cold water entered it from the mountain side, and then we went regularly into camp. We hired a large boat and two shot-guns from a lonely ranchman who lived some ten miles further on, and made ready for comfort and recreation. We soon got thoroughly acquainted with the lake and all its peculiarities.

CHAPTER XXXVIII.

MONO LAKE lies in a lifeless, treeless, hideous desert, eight thousand feet above the level of the sea, and is guarded by mountains two thousand feet higher, whose summits are always clothed in clouds. This solemn, silent, sailless sea — this lonely tenant of the loneliest spot on earth — is little graced with the picturesque. It is an unpretending expanse of grayish water, about a hundred miles in circumference, with two islands in its center, mere upheavals of rent and scorched and blistered lava, snowed over with gray banks and drifts of pumice-stone and ashes, the winding sheet of the dead volcano, whose vast crater the lake has seized upon and occupied.

The lake is two hundred feet deep, and its sluggish waters are so strong with alkali that if you only dip the most hopelessly soiled garment into them once or twice, and wring it out, it will be found as clean as if it had been through the ablest of washer-women's hands. While we camped there our laundry work was easy. We tied the week's washing astern of our boat, and sailed a quarter of a mile, and the job was complete, all to the wringing out.

If we threw the water on our heads and gave them
a rub or so, the white lather would pile up three
inches high. This water is not good for bruised
places and abrasions of the skin. We had a valuable dog. He had raw places on him. He had
more raw places on him than sound ones. He was
the rawest dog I almost ever saw. He jumped
overboard one day to get away from the flies. But
it was bad judgment. In his condition, it would
have been just as comfortable to jump into the fire.
The alkali water nipped him in all the raw places
simultaneously, and he struck out for the shore with
considerable interest. He yelped and barked and
howled as he went — and by the time he got to the
shore there was no bark to him — for he had barked
the bark all out of his inside, and the alkali water
had cleaned the bark all off his outside, and he
probably wished he had never embarked in any such
enterprise. He ran round and round in a circle,
and pawed the earth and clawed the air, and threw
double somersaults, sometimes backward and sometimes forward, in the most extraordinary manner.
He was not a demonstrative dog, as a general thing,
but rather of a grave and serious turn of mind, and
I never saw him take so much interest in anything
before. He finally struck out over the mountains,
at a gait which we estimated at about two hundred
and fifty miles an hour, and he is going yet. This
was about nine years ago. We look for what is left
of him along here every day.

A white man cannot drink the water of Mono
Lake, for it is nearly pure lye. It is said that the
Indians in the vicinity drink it sometimes, though.
It is not improbable, for they are among the purest
liars I ever saw. [There will be no additional
charge for this joke, except to parties requiring an
explanation of it. This joke has received high com-
mendation from some of the ablest minds of the
age.]

There are no fish in Mono Lake — no frogs, no
snakes, no polliwogs — nothing, in fact, that goes tc
make life desirable. Millions of wild ducks and sea-
gulls swim about the surface, but no living thing
exists *under* the surface, except a white feathery sort
of worm, one-half an inch long, which looks like a
bit of white thread frayed out at the sides. If you
dip up a gallon of water, you will get about fifteen
thousand of these. They give to the water a sort of
grayish-white appearance. Then there is a fly,
which looks something like our house fly. These
settle on the beach to eat the worms that wash
ashore — and any time, you can see there a belt of
flies an inch deep and six feet wide, and this belt
extends clear around the lake — a belt of flies one
hundred miles long. If you throw a stone among
them, they swarm up so thick that they look dense,
like a cloud. You can hold them under water as
long as you please — they do not mind it — they are
only proud of it. When you let them go, they pop
up to the surface as dry as a patent-office report,

and walk off as unconcernedly as if they had been educated especially with a view to affording instructive entertainment to man in that particular way. Providence leaves nothing to go by chance. All things have their uses and their part and proper place in Nature's economy: the ducks eat the flies — the flies eat the worms — the Indians eat all three — the wild cats eat the Indians — the white folks eat the wild cats — and thus all things are lovely.

Mono Lake is a hundred miles in a straight line from the ocean — and between it and the ocean are one or two ranges of mountains — yet thousands of sea-gulls go there every season to lay their eggs and rear their young. One would as soon expect to find sea-gulls in Kansas. And in this connection let us observe another instance of Nature's wisdom. The islands in the lake being merely huge masses of lava, coated over with ashes and pumice-stone, and utterly innocent of vegetation or anything that would burn; and sea-gulls' eggs being entirely useless to anybody unless they be cooked, Nature has provided an unfailing spring of boiling water on the largest island, and you can put your eggs in there, and in four minutes you can boil them as hard as any statement I have made during the past fifteen years. Within ten feet of the boiling spring is a spring of pure cold water, sweet and wholesome. So, in that island you get your board and washing free of charge — and if nature had gone further and furnished a nice American hotel clerk who was crusty and disobliging, and didn't know anything about the time tables, or the railroad routes — or — anything — and was proud of it — I would not wish for a more desirable boarding-house.

Half a dozen little mountain brooks flow into Mono Lake, but *not a stream of any kind flows out of it*. It neither rises nor falls, apparently, and what it does with its surplus water is a dark and bloody mystery.

There are only two seasons in the region round about Mono Lake — and these are, the breaking up of one winter and the beginning of the next. More than once (in Esmeralda) I have seen a perfectly blistering morning open up with the thermometer at ninety degrees at eight o'clock, and seen the snow fall fourteen inches deep and that same identical thermometer go down to forty-four degrees under shelter, before nine o'clock at night. Under favorable circumstances it snows at least once in every single month in the year, in the little town of Mono. So uncertain is the climate in summer that a lady who goes out visiting cannot hope to be prepared for all emergencies unless she takes her fan under one arm and her snow shoes under the other. When they have a Fourth of July procession it generally snows on them, and they do say that as a general thing when a man calls for a brandy toddy there, the barkeeper chops it off with a hatchet and wraps it up in a paper, like maple sugar. And it is further reported that the old soakers haven't any teeth — wore them out eating gin cocktails and brandy punches. I do not endorse that statement — I simply give it for what it is worth — and it is worth — well, I should say, millions, to any man who can believe it without straining himself. But I do endorse the snow on the Fourth of July — because I know that to be true.

20

CHAPTER XXXIX.

ABOUT seven o'clock one blistering hot morning — for it was now dead summer time — Higbie and I took the boat and started on a voyage of discovery to the two islands. We had often longed to do this, but had been deterred by the fear of storms; for they were frequent, and severe enough to capsize an ordinary rowboat like ours without great difficulty — and once capsized, death would ensue in spite of the bravest swimming, for that venomous water would eat a man's eyes out like fire, and burn him out inside, too, if he shipped a sea. It was called twelve miles, straight out to the islands — a long pull and a warm one — but the morning was so quiet and sunny, and the lake so smooth and glassy and dead, that we could not resist the temptation. So we filled two large tin canteens with water (since we were not acquainted with the locality of the spring said to exist on the large island), and started. Higbie's brawny muscles gave the boat good speed, but by the time we reached our destination we judged that we had pulled nearer fifteen miles than twelve.

We landed on the big island and went ashore. We tried the water in the canteens, now, and found that the sun had spoiled it; it was so brackish that we could not drink it; so we poured it out and began a search for the spring — for thirst augments fast as soon as it is apparent that one has no means at hand of quenching it. The island was a long, moderately high hill of ashes — nothing but gray ashes and pumice-stone, in which we sunk to our knees at every step — and all around the top was a forbidding wall of scorched and blasted rocks. When we reached the top and got within the wall, we found simply a shallow, far-reaching basin, carpeted with ashes, and here and there a patch of fine sand. In places, picturesque jets of steam shot up out of crevices, giving evidence that although this ancient crater had gone out of active business, there was still some fire left in its furnaces. Close to one of these jets of steam stood the only tree on the island — a small pine of most graceful shape and most faultless symmetry; its color was a brilliant green, for the steam drifted unceasingly through its branches and kept them always moist. It contrasted strangely enough, did this vigorous and beautiful outcast, with its dead and dismal surroundings. It was like a cheerful spirit in a mourning household.

We hunted for the spring everywhere, traversing the full length of the island (two or three miles), and crossing it twice — climbing ash-hills patiently, and then sliding down the other side in a sitting posture, plowing up smothering volumes of gray dust. But we found nothing but solitude, ashes, and a heart-breaking silence. Finally we noticed that the wind had risen, and we forgot our thirst in a solicitude of greater importance; for, the lake being quiet, we had not taken pains about securing the boat. We hurried back to a point overlooking our landing place, and then — but mere words cannot describe our dismay — the boat was gone! The chances were that there was not another boat on the entire lake. The situation was not comfortable — in truth, to speak plainly, it was frightful. We were prisoners on a desolate island, in aggravating proximity to friends who were for the present helpless to aid us; and what was still more uncomfortable was the reflection that we had neither food nor water. But presently we sighted the boat. It was drifting along, leisurely, about fifty yards from shore, tossing in a foamy sea. It drifted, and continued to drift, but at the same safe distance from land, and we walked along abreast it and waited for fortune to favor us. At the end of an hour it approached a jutting cape, and Higbie ran ahead and posted himself on the utmost verge and prepared for the assault. If we failed there, there was no hope for us. It was driving gradually shoreward all the time, now; but whether it was driving fast enough to make the connection or not was the momentous question. When it got within thirty steps of Higbie I was so excited that I fancied I could hear my own heart beat.   When, a little later, it dragged slowly along and seemed about to go by, only one little yard out of reach, it seemed as if my heart stood still; and when it was exactly abreast him and began to widen away, and he still standing like a watching statue, I knew my heart did stop. But when he gave a great spring, the next instant, and lit fairly in the stern, I discharged a war-whoop that awoke the solitudes!

But it dulled my enthusiasm, presently, when he told me he had not been caring whether the boat came within jumping distance or not, so that it passed within eight or ten yards of him, for he had made up his mind to shut his eyes and mouth and swim that trifling distance.   Imbecile that I was, I had not thought of that.   It was only a long swim that could be fatal.

The sea was running high and the storm increasing.   It was growing late, too — three or four in the afternoon.   Whether to venture toward the mainland or not, was a question of some moment.   But we were so distressed by thirst that we decided to try it, and so Higbie fell to work and I took the steering-oar.   When we had pulled a mile, laboriously, we were evidently in serious peril, for the storm had greatly augmented; the billows ran very high and were capped with foaming crests, the heavens were hung with black, and the wind blew with great fury. We would have gone back, now, but we did not dare to turn the boat around, because as soon as she got

in the trough of the sea she would upset, of course.
Our only hope lay in keeping her head-on to the
seas.   It was hard work to do this, she plunged so,
and so beat and belabored the billows with her rising
and falling bows.   Now and then one of Higbie's
oars would trip on the top of a wave, and the other
one would snatch the boat half around in spite of
my cumbersome steering apparatus.   We were
drenched by the sprays constantly, and the boat
occasionally shipped water.   By and by, powerful
as my comrade was, his great exertions began to
tell on him, and he was anxious that I should change
places with him till he could rest a little.   But I told
him this was impossible; for if the steering oar were
dropped a moment while we changed, the boat would
slue around into the trough of the sea, capsize, and
in less than five minutes we would have a hundred
gallons of soapsuds in us and be eaten up so quickly
that we could not even be present at our own inquest.

But things cannot last always.   Just as the darkness shut down we came booming into port, head
on.   Higbie dropped his oars to hurrah — I dropped
mine to help — the sea gave the boat a twist, and
over she went!

The agony that alkali water inflicts on bruises,
chafes, and blistered hands, is unspeakable, and
nothing but greasing all over will modify it — but
we ate, drank, and slept well, that night, notwithstanding.

In speaking of the peculiarities of Mono Lake, I

ought to have mentioned that at intervals all around its shores stand picturesque turret-looking masses and clusters of a whitish, coarse-grained rock that resembles inferior mortar dried hard; and if one breaks off fragments of this rock he will find perfectly shaped and thoroughly petrified gulls' eggs deeply imbedded in the mass. How did they get there? I simply state the fact — for it is a fact — and leave the geological reader to crack the nut at his leisure and solve the problem after his own fashion.

At the end of a week we adjourned to the Sierras on a fishing excursion, and spent several days in camp under snowy Castle Peak, and fished successfully for trout in a bright, miniature lake whose surface was between ten and eleven thousand feet above the level of the sea; cooling ourselves during the hot August noons by sitting on snowbanks ten feet deep, under whose sheltering edges *fine grass and dainty flowers flourished luxuriously;* and at night entertaining ourselves by almost freezing to death. Then we returned to Mono Lake, and finding that the cement excitement was over for the present, packed up and went back to Esmeralda. Mr. Ballou reconnoitered awhile, and not liking the prospect, set out alone for Humboldt.

About this time occurred a little incident which has always had a sort of interest to me, from the fact that it came so near "instigating" my funeral. At a time when an Indian attack had been expected, the citizens hid their gunpowder where it would be safe and yet convenient to hand when wanted. A neighbor of ours hid six cans of rifle powder in the bake-oven of an old discarded cooking stove which stood on the open ground near a frame outhouse or shed, and from and after that day never thought of it again. We hired a half-tamed Indian to do some washing for us, and he took up quarters under the shed with his tub. The ancient stove reposed within six feet of him, and before his face. Finally it occurred to him that hot water would be better than cold, and he went out and fired up under that forgotten powder magazine and set on a kettle of water. Then he returned to his tub. I entered the shed presently and threw down some more clothes, and was about to speak to him when the stove blew up with a prodigious crash, and disappeared, leaving not a splinter behind. Fragments of it fell in the streets full two hundred yards away. Nearly a third of the shed roof over our heads was destroyed, and one of the stove lids, after cutting a small stanchion half in two in front of the Indian, whizzed between us and drove partly through the weather-boarding beyond. I was as white as a sheet and as weak as a kitten and speechless. But the Indian betrayed no trepidation, no distress, not even discomfort. He simply stopped washing, leaned forward and surveyed the clean, blank ground a moment, and then remarked:

"Mph! Dam stove heap gone!"—and resumed his scrubbing as placidly as if it were an entirely customary thing for a stove to do. I will explain, that " heap " is " Injun-English " for " very much." The reader will perceive the exhaustive expressiveness of it in the present instance.

CHAPTER XL.

I NOW come to a curious episode — the most curious, I think, that had yet accented my slothful, valueless, heedless career. Out of a hillside toward the upper end of the town, projected a wall of reddish looking quartz-croppings, the exposed comb of a silver-bearing ledge that extended deep down into the earth, of course. It was owned by a company entitled the "Wide West." There was a shaft sixty or seventy feet deep on the under side of the croppings, and everybody was acquainted with the rock that came from it — and tolerably rich rock it was, too, but nothing extraordinary. I will remark here, that although to the inexperienced stranger all the quartz of a particular "district" looks about alike, an old resident of the camp can take a glance at a mixed pile of rock, separate the fragments and tell you which mine each came from, as easily as a confectioner can separate and classify the various kinds and qualities of candy in a mixed heap of the article.

All at once the town was thrown into a state of extraordinary excitement. In mining parlance the

Wide West had "struck it rich!" Everybody went
to see the new developments, and for some days
there was such a crowd of people about the Wide
West shaft that a stranger would have supposed
there was a mass meeting in session there. No
other topic was discussed but the rich strike, and
nobody thought or dreamed about anything else.
Every man brought away a specimen, ground it up
in a hand mortar, washed it out in his horn spoon,
and glared speechless upon the marvelous result.
It was not hard rock, but black, decomposed stuff
which could be crumbled in the hand like a baked
potato, and when spread out on a paper exhibited a
thick sprinkling of gold and particles of "native"
silver. Higbie brought a handful to the cabin, and
when he had washed it out his amazement was beyond description. Wide West stock soared sky-
wards. It was said that repeated offers had been
made for it at a thousand dollars a foot, and
promptly refused. We have all had the "blues"
— the mere skyblues — but mine were indigo,
now — because I did not own in the Wide West.
The world seemed hollow to me, and existence a
grief. I lost my appetite, and ceased to take an
interest in anything. Still I had to stay, and listen
to other people's rejoicings, because I had no money
to get out of the camp with.

The Wide West company put a stop to the carrying away of "specimens," and well they might, for
every handful of the ore was worth a sum of some

consequence. To show the exceeding value of the ore, I will remark that a sixteen-hundred-pounds parcel of it was sold, just as it lay, at the mouth of the shaft, at *one dollar a pound;* and the man who bought it " packed " it on mules a hundred and fifty or two hundred miles, over the mountains, to San Francisco, satisfied that it would yield at a rate that would richly compensate him for his trouble. The Wide West people also commanded their foreman to refuse any but their own operatives permission to enter the mine at any time or for any purpose. I kept up my " blue " meditations and Higbie kept up a deal of thinking, too, but of a different sort. He puzzled over the " rock," examined it with a glass, inspected it in different lights and from different points of view, and after each experiment delivered himself, in soliloquy, of one and the same unvarying opinion in the same unvarying formula:

" It is *not* Wide West rock!"

He said once or twice that he meant to have a look into the Wide West shaft if he got shot for it. I was wretched, and did not care whether he got a look into it or not. He failed that day, and tried again at night; failed again; got up at dawn and tried, and failed again. Then he lay in ambush in the sage-brush hour after hour, waiting for the two or three hands to adjourn to the shade of a boulder for dinner; made a start once, but was premature — one of the men came back for something; tried it again, but when almost at the mouth of the shaft, another of the men rose up from behind the boulder as if to reconnoitre, and he dropped on the ground and lay quiet; presently he crawled on his hands and knees to the mouth of the shaft, gave a quick glance around, then seized the rope and slid down the shaft. He disappeared in the gloom of a " side drift " just as a head appeared in the mouth of the shaft and somebody shouted " Hello !"— which he did not answer. He was not disturbed any more. An hour later he entered the cabin, hot, red, and ready to burst with smothered excitement, and exclaimed in a stage whisper:

" I knew it ! We are rich ! IT'S A BLIND LEAD !"

I thought the very earth reeled under me. Doubt — conviction — doubt again — exultation — hope, amazement, belief, unbelief — every emotion imaginable swept in wild procession through my heart and brain, and I could not speak a word. After a moment or two of this mental fury, I shook myself to rights, and said:

" Say it again !"

" It's a blind lead !"

" Cal., let's — let's burn the house — or kill somebody ! Let's get out where there's room to hurrah ! But what is the use? It is a hundred times too good to be true."

" It's a blind lead for a million !— hanging wall — foot wall — clay casings — everything complete !" He swung his hat and gave three cheers, and I cast

doubt to the winds and chimed in with a will. For
I was worth a million dollars, and did not care
' whether school kept or not !''

But perhaps I ought to explain. A " blind lead "
is a lead or ledge that does not " crop out " above
the surface. A miner does not know where to look
for such leads, but they are often stumbled upon by
accident in the course of driving a tunnel or sinking
a shaft. Higbie knew the Wide West rock perfectly
well, and the more he had examined the new
developments the more he was satisfied that the ore
could not have come from the Wide West vein.
And so had it occurred to him alone, of all the
camp, that there was a blind lead down in the shaft,
and that even the Wide West people themselves did
not suspect it. He was right. When he went down
the shaft, he found that the blind lead held its independent way through the Wide West vein, cutting it
diagonally, and that it was enclosed in its own well-
defined casing-rocks and clay. Hence it was public
property. Both leads being perfectly well defined,
it was easy for any miner to see which one belonged
to the Wide West and which did not.

We thought it well to have a strong friend, and
therefore we brought the foreman of the Wide West
to our cabin that night and revealed the great surprise to him. Higbie said:

" We are going to take possession of this blind
lead, record it and establish ownership, and then
forbid the Wide West company to take out any

more of the rock. You cannot help your company in this matter — nobody can help them. I will go into the shaft with you and prove to your entire satisfaction that it *is* a blind lead. Now we propose to take you in with us, and claim the blind lead in our three names. What do you say?"

What could a man say who had an opportunity to simply stretch forth his hand and take possession of a fortune without risk of any kind and without wronging any one or attaching the least taint of dishonor to his name? He could only say, " Agreed."

The notice was put up that night, and duly spread upon the recorder's books before ten o'clock. We claimed two hundred feet each — six hundred feet in all — the smallest and compactest organization in the district, and the easiest to manage.

No one can be so thoughtless as to suppose that we slept that night. Higbie and I went to bed at midnight, but it was only to lie broad awake and think, dream, scheme. The floorless, tumble-down cabin was a palace, the ragged gray blankets silk, the furniture rosewood and mahogany. Each new splendor that burst out of my visions of the future whirled me bodily over in bed or jerked me to a sitting posture just as if an electric battery had been applied to me. We shot fragments of conversation back and forth at each other. Once Higbie said:

" When are you going home — to the States?"

" To-morrow!"— with an evolution or two, end-ing with a sitting position. "Well — no — but next month, at furthest."

"We'll go in the same steamer."

"Agreed."

A pause.

"Steamer of the 10th?"

"Yes. No, the 1st."

"All right."

Another pause.

"Where are you going to live?" said Higbie.

"San Francisco."

"That's me!"

Pause.

"Too high — too much climbing "— from Higbie.

"What is?"

"I was thinking of Russian Hill — building a house up there."

"Too much climbing? Shan't you keep a carriage?"

"Of course. I forgot that."

Pause.

"Cal., what kind of a house are you going to build?"

"I was thinking about that. Three-story and an attic."

"But what *kind?*"

"Well, I don't hardly know. Brick, I suppose."

"Brick — bosh."

"Why? What is your idea?"

"Brown - stone front — French plate glass —

billiard-room off the dining-room — statuary and
paintings — shrubbery and two-acre grass plat —
greenhouse — iron dog on the front stoop — gray
horses — landau, and a coachman with a bug on his
hat !''

'' By George !''

A long pause.

'' Cal., when are you going to Europe?''

'' Well — I hadn't thought of that. When are
you?''

'' In the spring.''

'' Going to be gone all summer?''

'' All summer ! I shall remain there three years.''

'' No — but are you in earnest?''

'' Indeed I am.''

'' I will go along too.''

'' Why of course you will.''

'' What part of Europe shall you go to?''

'' All parts. France, England, Germany — Spain,
Italy, Switzerland, Syria, Greece, Palestine, Arabia,
Persia, Egypt — all over — everywhere.''

'' I'm agreed.''

'' All right.''

'' Won't it be a swell trip !''

'' We'll spend forty or fifty thousand dollars trying to make it one, anyway.''

Another long pause.

'' Higbie, we owe the butcher six dollars, and he
has been threatening to stop our —''

'' Hang the butcher !''

21

" Amen."

And so it went on. By three o'clock we found it was no use, and so we got up and played cribbage and smoked pipes till sunrise. It was my week to cook. I always hated cooking — now, I abhorred it.

The news was all over town. The former excitement was great — this one was greater still. I walked the streets serene and happy. Higbie said the foreman had been offered two hundred thousand dollars for his third of the mine. I said I would like to see myself selling for any such price. My ideas were lofty. My figure was a million. Still, I honestly believe that if I had been offered it, it would have had no other effect than to make me hold off for more.

I found abundant enjoyment in being rich. A man offered me a three-hundred-dollar horse, and wanted to take my simple, unendorsed note for it. That brought the most realizing sense I had yet had that I was actually rich, beyond shadow of doubt. It was followed by numerous other evidences of a similar nature — among which I may mention the fact of the butcher leaving us a double supply of meat and saying nothing about money.

By the laws of the district, the " locators " or claimants of a ledge were obliged to do a fair and reasonable amount of work on their new property within ten days after the date of the location, or the property was forfeited, and anybody could go and seize it that chose. So we determined to go to work the next day. About the middle of the afternoon, as I was coming out of the post-office, I met a Mr. Gardiner, who told me that Capt. John Nye was lying dangerously ill at his place (the "Nine-Mile Ranch"), and that he and his wife were not able to give him nearly as much care and attention as his case demanded. I said if he would wait for me a moment, I would go down and help in the sick room. I ran to the cabin to tell Higbie. He was not there, but I left a note on the table for him, and a few minutes later I left town in Gardiner's wagon.

CHAPTER XLI.

CAPTAIN NYE was very ill indeed, with spasmodic rheumatism. But the old gentleman was himself — which is to say, he was kind-hearted and agreeable when comfortable, but a singularly violent wildcat when things did not go well. He would be smiling along pleasantly enough, when a sudden spasm of his disease would take him and he would go out of his smile into a perfect fury. He would groan and wail and howl with the anguish, and fill up the odd chinks with the most elaborate profanity that strong convictions and a fine fancy could contrive. With fair opportunity he could swear very well and handle his adjectives with considerable judgment; but when the spasm was on him it was painful to listen to him, he was so awkward. However, I had seen him nurse a sick man himself and put up patiently with the inconveniences of the situation, and consequently I was willing that he should have full license now that his own turn had come. He could not disturb me, with all his raving and ranting, for my mind had work on hand, and it labored on diligently, night and day, whether

my hands were idle or employed. I was altering
and amending the plans for my house, and thinking
over the propriety of having the billiard-room in the
attic, instead of on the same floor with the dining-
room; also, I was trying to decide between green
and blue for the upholstery of the drawing-room,
for, although my preference was blue I feared it was
a color that would be too easily damaged by dust
and sunlight; likewise while I was content to put
the coachman in a modest livery, I was uncertain
about a footman — I needed one, and was even resolved to have one, but wished he could properly
appear and perform his functions out of livery, for
I somewhat dreaded so much show; and yet, inas-
much as my late grandfather had had a coachman
and such things, but no liveries, I felt rather drawn
to beat him; — or beat his ghost, at any rate; I was
also systematizing the European trip, and managed
to get it all laid out, as to route and length of time
to be devoted to it — everything, with one exception
— namely, whether to cross the desert from Cairo
to Jerusalem per camel, or go by sea to Beirut, and
thence down through the country per caravan.
Meantime I was writing to the friends at home every
day, instructing them concerning all my plans and
intentions, and directing them to look up a handsome homestead for my mother and agree upon a
price for it against my coming, and also directing
them to sell my share of the Tennessee land and
tender the proceeds to the widows' and orphans'

fund of the typographical union of which I had long
been a member in good standing. [This Tennessee
land had been in the possession of the family many
years, and promised to confer high fortune upon us
some day; it still promises it, but in a less violent
way.]

When I had been nursing the Captain nine days
he was somewhat better, but very feeble. During
the afternoon we lifted him into a chair and gave
him an alcoholic vapor bath, and then set about
putting him on the bed again. We had to be exceedingly careful, for the least jar produced pain.
Gardiner had his shoulders and I his legs; in an
unfortunate moment I stumbled and the patient fell
heavily on the bed in an agony of torture. I never
heard a man swear so in my life. He raved like a
maniac, and tried to snatch a revolver from the
table — but I got it. He ordered me out of the
house, and swore a world of oaths that he would kill
me wherever he caught me when he got on his feet
again. It was simply a passing fury, and meant
nothing. I knew he would forget it in an hour, and
maybe be sorry for it, too; but it angered me a
little, at the moment. So much so, indeed, that I
determined to go back to Esmeralda. I thought
he was able to get along alone, now, since he was
on the warpath. I took supper, and as soon as the
moon rose, began my nine-mile journey, on foot.
Even millionaires needed no horses, in those days,
for a mere nine-mile jaunt without baggage.

As I "raised the hill" overlooking the town, it lacked fifteen minutes of twelve. I glanced at the hill over beyond the canyon, and in the bright moonlight saw what appeared to be about half the population of the village massed on and around the Wide West croppings. My heart gave an exulting bound, and I said to myself, "They have made a new strike to-night — and struck it richer than ever, no doubt." I started over there, but gave it up. I said the "strike" would keep, and I had climbed hills enough for one night. I went on down through the town, and as I was passing a little German bakery, a woman ran out and begged me to come in and help her. She said her husband had a fit. I went in, and judged she was right — he appeared to have a hundred of them, compressed into one. Two Germans were there, trying to hold him, and not making much of a success of it. I ran up the street half a block or so and routed out a sleeping doctor, brought him down half dressed, and we four wrestled with the maniac, and doctored, drenched and bled him, for more than an hour, and the poor German woman did the crying. He grew quiet, now, and the doctor and I withdrew and left him to his friends.

It was a little after one o'clock. As I entered the cabin door, tired but jolly, the dingy light of a tallow candle revealed Higbie, sitting by the pine table gazing stupidly at my note, which he held in his fingers, and looking pale, old, and haggard. I

21*

halted, and looked at him. He looked at me,
stolidly. I said:

"Higbie, what—what is it?"

"We're ruined — we didn't do the work — THE
BLIND LEAD'S RELOCATED!"

It was enough. I sat down sick, grieved —
broken-hearted, indeed. A minute before, I was rich
and brimful of vanity; I was a pauper now, and
very meek. We sat still an hour, busy with thought,
busy with vain and useless self-upbraidings, busy
with "Why *didn't* I do this, and why *didn't* I do
that," but neither spoke a word. Then we dropped
into mutual explanations, and the mystery was
cleared away. It came out that Higbie had de-
pended on me, as I had on him, and as both of us
had on the foreman. The folly of it! It was the
first time that ever staid and steadfast Higbie had
left an important matter to chance or failed to be
true to his full share of a responsibility.

But he had never seen my note till this moment,
and this moment was the first time he had been in
the cabin since the day he had seen me last. He,
also, had left a note for me, on that same fatal afternoon — had ridden up on horseback, and looked
through the window, and being in a hurry and not
seeing me, had tossed the note into the cabin
through a broken pane. Here it was, on the floor,
where it had remained undisturbed for nine days:

"Don't fail to do the work before the ten days expire. W. has
passed through and given me notice. I am to join him at Mono Lake,

and we shall go on from there to-night.   He says he will find it this
time, sure.   CAL."

"W." meant Whiteman, of course.   That thrice
accursed "cement"!

That was the way of it.   An old miner, like
Higbie, could no more withstand the fascination of
a mysterious mining excitement like this "cement"
foolishness, than he could refrain from eating when
he was famishing.   Higbie had been dreaming about
the marvelous cement for months; and now, against
his better judgment, he had gone off and "taken
the chances" on my keeping secure a mine worth a
million undiscovered cement veins.   They had not
been followed this time.   His riding out of town in
broad daylight was such a commonplace thing to do
that it had not attracted any attention.   He said they
prosecuted their search in the fastnesses of the
mountains during nine days, without success; they
could not find the cement.   Then a ghastly fear
came over him that something might have happened
to prevent the doing of the necessary work to hold
the blind lead (though indeed he thought such a
thing hardly possible) and forthwith he started
home with all speed.   He would have reached
Esmeralda in time, but his horse broke down and he
had to walk a great part of the distance.   And so it
happened that as he came into Esmeralda by one
road, I entered it by another.   His was the superior
energy, however, for he went straight to the Wide
West, instead of turning aside as I had done — and

U*

he arrived there about five or ten minutes too late!
The "notice" was already up, the "relocation"
of our mine completed beyond recall, and the crowd
rapidly dispersing. He learned some facts before
he left the ground. The foreman had not been
seen about the streets since the night we had located
the mine — a telegram had called him to California
on a matter of life and death, it was said. At any
rate he had done no work and the watchful eyes of
the community were taking note of the fact. At
midnight of this woful tenth day, the ledge would
be "relocatable," and by eleven o'clock the hill
was black with men prepared to do the relocating.
That was the crowd I had seen when I fancied a
new "strike" had been made — idiot that I was.
[We three had the same right to relocate the lead
that other people had, provided we were quick
enough.] As midnight was announced, fourteen
men, duly armed and ready to back their proceedings, put up their "notice" and proclaimed their
ownership of the blind lead, under the new name of
the "Johnson." But A. D. Allen, our partner (the
foreman), put in a sudden appearance about that
time, with a cocked revolver in his hand, and said
his name must be added to the list, or he would
"thin out the Johnson company some." He was
a manly, splendid, determined fellow, and known to
be as good as his word, and therefore a compromise
was effected. They put in his name for a hundred
feet, reserving to themselves the customary two

hundred feet each. Such was the history of the night's events, as Higbie gathered from a friend on the way home.

Higbie and I cleared out on a new mining excitement the next morning, glad to get away from the scene of our sufferings, and after a month or two of hardship and disappointment, returned to Esmeralda once more. Then we learned that the Wide West and the Johnson companies had consolidated; that the stock, thus united, comprised five thousand feet, or shares; that the foreman, apprehending tiresome litigation, and considering such a huge concern unwieldy, had sold his hundred feet for ninety thousand dollars in gold and gone home to the States to enjoy it. If the stock was worth such a gallant figure, with five thousand shares in the corporation, it makes me dizzy to think what it would have been worth with only our original six hundred in it. It was the difference between six hundred men owning a house and five thousand owning it. We would have been millionaires if we had only worked with pick and spade one little day on our property and so secured our ownership!

It reads like a wild fancy sketch, but the evidence of many witnesses, and likewise that of the official records of Esmeralda District, is easily obtainable in proof that it is a true history. I can always have it to say that I was absolutely and unquestionably worth a million dollars, once, for ten days.

A year ago my esteemed and in every way estimable old millionaire partner, Higbie, wrote me from an obscure little mining camp in California that after nine or ten years of buffetings and hard striving, he was at last in a position where he could command twenty-five hundred dollars, and said he meant to go into the fruit business in a modest way. How such a thought would have insulted him the night we lay in our cabin planning European trips and brown-stone houses on Russian Hill!

P